Contents

D1328711

Acknowledgements

As editor, I would like to thank the contributors to this book for making time available to work up their material in a climate where there are many competing claims on their time and energy, and for doing all this without financial reward; the royalties from this volume will go to the Tavistock Institute of Medical Psychology, a charitable body. I would also like to thank Joanna Moriarty who, as commissioning editor, encouraged me to go ahead with the project at a time when it would have been very easy for other commitments to take priority.

Jane Simpson acknowledges the help of Elizabeth Spillett who did much of the research for Chapter 2. Sue Walrond-Skinner thanks Canon David Atkinson, Chancellor of Southwark Cathedral, for helping her think through some ideas about covenant which appear in Chapter 3. I am very grateful to Cesare Sacerdoti of Karnac Books for permission to reprint Martin Richards' contribution in Chapter 5. This was first published in almost identical form under the title 'Learning from divorce' in Clulow, C. (ed.) *Rethinking Marriage: Public and Private Perspectives*. London: Karnac Books 1993. Robert Morley acknowledges the helpful comments on Chapter 6 from his wife, Elspeth Morley, and from Barbara Dearnley, Haddie Davis, Carole Shelton and members of the Applied Group of the British Association of Psychotherapists.

Christopher Clulow

Biographical Notes

Ceridwen Roberts is Director of the Family Policy Studies Centre in London. A sociologist, she was Principal Research Officer in the Employment Department, where she worked for 14 years. She began her career as a lecturer at Trent Polytechnic. Her current interest in family policy and research stems from earlier work on the position of women in the labour market. Together with Jean Martin she wrote *Women and Employment – A Lifetime Perspective*, and has subsequently worked on many aspects of labour market flexibility. At the Family Policy Studies Centre she is developing research on the changing structure and nature of families in Britain, extending the Centre's comparative work and continuing the focus on European development. She leads the Centre's work in promoting informed discussion of the changing structure of families in Britain and the implications for policy. She was also recently involved in the United Kingdom Association for the International Year of the Family and in a programme of events to mark the year.

Jane Simpson was born in London and educated at Channing School, Highgate, and University College, London, where she met her husband Alasdair. They qualified as solicitors in 1967 and their first child was born in 1968. She took extended maternity leave, during which time she had a second daughter and a son, and trained as a marriage guidance counsellor. She returned to law in 1977 to start a family law department at Manches and Company, the firm where she currently works. In 1982 she co-founded the Solicitors Family Law Association which she now chairs. The Association has some 3,500 members, who aim to guide their clients towards fair, negotiated settlements, rather than those imposed by courts. She is also actively involved in the management of the recently formed Tavistock and Portman Clinics National Health Service Trust.

Sue Walrond-Skinner is a family and marital therapist who has practised and written extensively in the field of family therapy, and who continues to practise and teach. She is also an Anglican priest, and is currently employed as Adviser in Pastoral Care and Counselling to the Diocese of Southwark. At present she is engaged in researching into the family life of clergy and the particular effects of the ordination of women to the priesthood on clergy marriages and families.

Stanley Ruszczynski is a Senior Marital Psychotherapist at the Tavistock Marital Studies Institute, London. After graduating from the London School of Economics he trained and worked as a social worker in a local authority social services department. He joined the Institute in 1979, contributing to its clinical, teaching and research activities. He is a past Deputy Director of the Institute, was Co-ordinator of Training and Consultation, and is a founding member of the Society of Psychoanalytical Marital Psychotherapists. He has published a number of papers, and contributed to and edited *Psychotherapy With Couples*. He is a full member of the British Association of Psychotherapists and practises privately as an individual psychoanalytic psychotherapist.

Martin Richards is Reader in Human Development at Cambridge University and Head of the Centre for Family Research (formerly the Child Care and Development Group). He has researched extensively in the areas of parent-child relations, and divorce and marriage. His books include *Sexual Arrangements: Marriage and Affairs* (with Janet Reibstein), *Divorce Matters* (with Jackie Burgoyne and Roger Ormrod), *Infancy: the World of the Newborn*, and *Children in Social Worlds* (edited with Paul Light).

Robert Morley trained as a probation officer after war service and graduation from Durham University, and was involved in the work of the Probation Service with the Matrimonial Jurisdiction of the Magistrates Courts. He supplemented this experience by training with the Family Discussion Bureau (now the Tavistock Marital Studies Institute) between 1958 and 1964, for part of which time he was a Casework Fellow. In 1967 he left the Probation Service to become Senior Lecturer (later Principal Lecturer) in Social Work at the Hatfield Polytechnic, developing the first degree course in the United Kingdom for social work. During this time he qualified as a psychotherapist with the British Association of Psychotherapists. He joined the (now) Tavistock Marital Studies Institute in 1973 as a senior staff member. He left in 1976 to become Director of the Family Welfare Association, a post which he held until retirement. He continues to practise as a marital and individual psychotherapist and to write about this work. He is the author of *Intimate Strangers*, a book on marital interaction.

Annette Lawson is a sociologist who works on the boundaries of psychology and other humanities and social science disciplines. Having held university posts in the United Kingdom and the United

States, she now works independently as a feminist scholar and equal opportunities consultant. An activist, she chairs the Women's Advisory Panel to the Opportunity 2000 Campaign on behalf of the Fawcett Society, and she is on the executive committees of the Women's Studies Network (United Kingdom) Association and of the National Alliance of Women's Organizations. She is the author of *Adultery: An Analysis of Love and Betrayal*. Her most recent scholarly work has been on adolescent sexuality, while, as a consultant, she is engaged on drafting the new plan of action on women and development for the Commonwealth Secretariat.

Mavis Maclean has been studying family law and social policy at the Centre for Socio-Legal Studies at Oxford University for over twenty years. She has taught and published extensively in this field, recent books including *Surviving Divorce* and, as a co-editor, *Family Politics and the Law*. She is married with two children.

Susie Orbach has a psychotherapy practice seeing individuals and couples. She co-founded the Women's Therapy Centre in London in 1976 and, in 1981, the Women's Therapy Centre Institute, a post-graduate training centre for psychotherapists in New York. She is the author of *Fat is a Feminist Issue, Fat is a Feminist Issue 2, Hunger Strike: The Anorectic's Struggle as a Metaphor For Our Age* and *What's Really Going On Here?* With Luise Eichenbaum she has written *Understanding Women: A Feminist Psychoanalytic Account, What Do Women Want: Exploding the Myth of Dependency*, and *Bittersweet: Love, Competition and Envy in Women's Relationships*. She writes a regular column on relationship issues for *Guardian Weekend*. She lives in London with her partner and their two children.

Sebastian Kraemer studied medicine, specializing in paediatrics and later in psychiatry, after taking a first degree in philosophy. Since 1980 he has been a Consultant Child and Family Psychiatrist at the Tavistock Clinic and at the Whittington Hospital, London. His principal interests and publications are in family therapy and psychosomatic disorders, the training of child and adolescent psychiatrists, and in the origins and roles of fatherhood. He has appeared in television programmes and published in the press on the subject of parenthood and its stresses for both men and women. He is married with two school-age sons.

Rosine Jozef Perelberg gained a doctorate in Social Anthropology at the London School of Economics. She worked at the Maudsley Hospital as a psychotherapist, and at the Marlborough Family

Service as Senior Psychotherapist and Family Therapist for many years. She is a Member of the Institute of Family Therapy and of the British Psychoanalytical Society. She is Associate Editor of the *New Library of Psychoanalysis* and co-editor of *Gender and Power in Families*. She works as a psychoanalyst in private practice and on a research project in London at the Anna Freud Centre on breakdown in young adulthood.

Christopher Clulow is Director of the Tavistock Marital Studies Institute, London, where he works as a marital psychotherapist, teacher and researcher. He has published extensively on marriage and family issues, his particular interests being the transition into parenthood and the management of divorce. His books include *To Have and To Hold: Marriage, The First Baby and Preparing Couples for Parenthood; Marital Therapy: An Inside View; In the Child's Best Interests?* (with Christopher Vincent); *Marriage Inside Out: Understanding Problems of Intimacy* (with Janet Mattinson) and, as editor, *Marriage, Disillusion and Hope* and *Rethinking Marriage: Public and Private Perspectives*. After graduating in Economics at the University of Exeter, he completed a post-graduate social work training and worked in the Probation Service for five years. He joined the Tavistock Marital Studies Institute in 1974, and from 1986–1994 chaired the Commission on Marriage and Interpersonal Relations of the International Union of Family Organizations. In 1993 he became a founding member of the Society of Psychoanalytical Marital Psychotherapists. He is married with two daughters.

| Introduction

Fragments of a Partnership

She is 32, a slight, attractive woman whose physical stature belies the drive she brings to the successful brokerage business she has built up over recent years. He is 34, a big man who works for himself as a furniture restorer. They have lived together for six years. They are not married and have no children.

She is talking. Why, she asks, does he need to ring her at work to ask what to buy for supper? Why can't he decide? Why does he always dump this kind of responsibility on her? Can't he just go out and buy something? His expression, at first impassive, slips momentarily to reveal a mixture of anger and hurt. He replies that he had thought he was helping, and she would only complain that he had bought the wrong food if he didn't consult her. She disagrees, but adds that even if he was right, it could hardly make matters worse in terms of the way things had worked out. What happened? He bought supper. She came home late from work and cooked it. He ate. She didn't. They sat in angry silence.

The trivia of domestic life provide a window on the big picture of marriage. But how are they to be understood? Depending on where you stand, the picture is likely to change: she sees a man who expects her to carry all the domestic responsibilities of their relationship on top of what she has to manage at work; he sees a woman who is quick to criticize him and who fails to appreciate the efforts he makes. Each longs for the other to support what they are doing. Each is disappointed, and has a different explanation for why things work out between them in the way they do.

Their therapist sees something different. Informed by past discussions and the context in which the incident is recounted, he sees another link in the chain of purposive misunderstandings that occur between them. Their longing to be cared for is countered by an equally powerful fear that they will be negated by the experience. Contrary to their conscious wishes, the barrier of misunderstanding protects them from a fear of being absorbed by each other.

The therapist regards their complaint as their contract: the fear of being bound together constituting part of what binds them together. The genesis of this contract he understands as being rooted in a past world of family experiences, causing each to peer into the murky waters of intimacy through very personalized spectacles. The man unconsciously associates his partner with a critical father who admonished him for being a 'waster', and who did not appreciate his achievements. The woman unconsciously associates her partner with a father whose attention was difficult to claim, making her doubt her value as a woman, and leaving her angry with seemingly indifferent, inaccessible men. Only women, as mothers, had compensated for the disappointment each of them had felt towards men, as fathers. As a man, their therapist wonders how far he will be able to break the mould.

Social scientists might observe that the tensions experienced and articulated by this couple are symptomatic of a general malaise in the relations between the sexes. They might argue that the woman in particular has every reason to be cautious about committing herself to marriage when the institution has played such a prominent part in discriminating against the interests of women to the advantage of men. The couple's cohabiting status might be regarded as the norm, and an understandable reaction against socially endorsed arrangements for intimacy in adult life which shackle rather than liberate women and men. Domestic squabbles about who does the shopping (or, more tellingly, who cleans the loo) are then understood as but one of many minor skirmishes in the general battle of the sexes over the gendered division of labour in society as a whole.

And a confused battle it can be. Politicians, concerned about spiralling public costs associated with high divorce rates and the growing number of lone-parent households, invoke 'basic' values to support policies that limit the claims on the public purse of personal decisions people take about their living arrangements. Church leaders, who might on moral grounds be expected to ally themselves with politicians on this issue, are to be found drawing the attention of government to its responsibility for managing the socio-economic landscape of the community in ways that do not marginalize its most vulnerable members.

Public commentators call for clarification from 'experts' about what is happening to marriage and family life. Liberal parents adapt to the independence and sexual freedom of their children, but then wonder about the thresholds that distinguish 'good friends' from 'family' when the traditional markers of engagements and weddings are in retreat. The battle of the sexes can merge into conflicts between social structures and individual freedoms, between collective responsibilities and personal interests, the meanings of which change according to the level at which the discourse takes place.

Most of the skirmishing occurs behind the closed doors of people's homes, especially when partners feel trapped and imprisoned. Back in the therapeutic conversation, the man discloses that structures, for him, mean rules, to which he has an aversion. So he works for himself, avoids getting in too deep with his customers, and safeguards his independence and flexibility of movement in every way possible. Marriage, to him, smacks of being rule-bound, and is therefore to be avoided. Besides, his parents' marriage ended when he was a child. Why repeat that trauma and their mistakes? He recalls with a touch of irony that his father had been a stickler for rules. She laughs hollowly about his determination not to be rule-bound. He is the only man she has known who insists on the pans in the kitchen being stored in a particular order. While he is surrounded by seeming chaos, he knows where everything in the house is – provided she does not tidy up. Yet he knows she is an organizer, just as she knows he is not to be organized.

So the debate about the relationship between women and men goes on at different levels, pervading all areas of life. As far as marriage goes, the personal tie between the sexes is what is valued in contemporary industrial societies, not the social contract. Such public morality asserts that the *relationship* is paramount, something which is defined by individuals and not by legal status; that it is the foundation of the family unit and should be the couple's first priority; and that the pursuit of intimacy, sexual satisfaction and fulfilment within an egalitarian framework is the ideal (Burgoyne, 1991).

Within these parameters it could be said that our couple has a marriage, although one in which the realities of life contradict the aspirations of each partner. But if they have a marriage, what is the nature of their contract? By what rules is the relationship governed? And how do these mesh with what is happening around them? Like the shell of the house they have gutted for renovation, their 'marriage' is full of possibilities and problems. Will they break new ground, or turn out simply to have reinvented the wheel?

Auditing Marriage

The confusion women and men experience at a personal level about whether or not they have a marriage – and, if so, what kind of marriage – is replicated in the debate about marriage at the public level. High divorce rates, falling marriage rates, the increasing popularity of cohabitation and a rapid rise in the number of births occurring outside wedlock have led to predictions that the institution of marriage has had its day. Public attention has shifted away from a preoccupation with mending marriage towards attempting to ensure that broken marriages are given a decent burial.

If marriage is dead, it refuses to lie down. One of the more confusing statistics of recent years is that the UK not only comes second in the European Community divorce league table, but also has the second highest marriage rate. While there can be no divorce without marriage, this positioning suggests that people have not given up on marriage. But it also suggests that at the present time marriage is proving to be a problematic enterprise.

In these circumstances it is important to try and take stock of what is happening to marriage. In the market-oriented language of our times – which is perhaps not so inappropriate for an organization that has immense, if concealed, economic implications for individuals and society – the time has come to *audit* marriage. The starting point for such an exercise is to try to identify the different strands which tie couples together in this legally sanctioned, publically witnessed union of one man with one woman, voluntarily entered into, to the exclusion of all others, and with the intention of lifelong commitment. This is no straightforward job. Marriage is an open system, mediating between the private worlds of individuals and the social world of which they are a part. Any audit of marriage must take account of different perspectives, different realities and different levels of meaning – just as must any audit of a particular marriage.

It was with this in mind that the Tavistock Marital Studies Institute organized a series of public lectures at the Tavistock Centre, London, in the Spring of 1994, as its contribution to marking what the UN had designated as the International Year of the Family. Speakers from different professional backgrounds, all of them authorities in their particular field, were invited to address what they saw as the essential nature of marriage and to identify issues that it raised for individuals and society.

By this means it was intended to build up a picture of contemporary marriage, one that highlighted its different purposes and offered explanations for the problems it seems to be having. While the picture would be based on experiences within the UK, it was expected that it would have much in common with those of other countries in the so-called developed world. All the chapters in this book, bar one which was added at a later stage, are based on the lectures that were given in the series. Together they weave a complex tapestry that is marriage today. Many of the strands interlock, building up clear patterns and themes that tell a coherent story; others cut across and obscure images that were beginning to emerge, inviting questions rather than providing answers.

The tapestry is inevitably incomplete. Twelve chapters cannot give a comprehensive account of marriage. Perspectives not included in this collection would change the picture. Different contributors from the perspectives which are represented would provide different emphases and altered tonings. But the pictures painted in the chapters do tell a story: it is for the reader to decide how adequate and coherent that story is when pieced together as a whole. I have approached the editorial task in the spirit of assembling the story. What I hope I have achieved is a reasonably coherent narrative of contemporary marriage, one that moves in and out of private and public worlds while keeping them firmly connected with each other. Marriage is *par excellence* a threshold institution, mediating his and her experience of social and psychological realities through the relationship they have as a couple, and linking their world as a couple with the wider concerns of society.

The quality of the narrative is more circular than linear, viewing and reviewing similar themes from different angles. Conclusions, such as there are, are not hard and fast – the story is still unfolding. Like all stories, it will contain elements of fiction. But it will also contain some fundamental truths which speak to our present predicament and link us with the past. So it is in the spirit of reading a story that the reader is invited to engage with what follows.

Outline for a Story

If you cannot begin at the beginning, the best place to start from is where you happen to be at the moment. We happen to be at a point in history where some people are asking if marriage is a thing of the past. It is not the first time this question has been asked, nor will it be the last. But it often feels as if it is the first time, and a pervasive sense of disquiet can make us believe that marriage is in a state of crisis – not, as has been observed, that marriage *is* a state of crisis, always and inevitably challenged by forces from inside and outside the partnership.

The problem with starting from where you are is that you can be tempted to believe that the whole story is contained in the picture you see at any one particular time, discounting things that might have been the same (or different) in the past, and those that might be different (or the same) in the future. The error is rather similar to taking a frame of videotape and believing it constitutes the whole film.

Ceridwen Roberts cautions against this tendency as she presents, in Chapter 1, a statistical picture of what is happening to marriage in this and other European countries at the present time. She addresses the anxiety that lies behind the current debate about marriage, pointing out that fears associated with changes taking place within society as a whole often find expression in the public debate about marriage and family life. This process at the 'macro' level of social organization is not dissimilar to the dynamic processes operating at the 'micro' level between couples. Symptoms can be constructed to sign dis-ease in one area of a person's life when it is actually sited elsewhere. The analogy is also apposite for the panic couples can feel in a crisis when memories of having survived similar experiences in the past and the fact that life will go on in the future can be obliterated. Crises have a habit of polarizing images of marriage into the very positive or the very negative, a theme that Stanley Ruszczynski develops at the 'micro' level later on.

From her review, Roberts concludes that announcements of the demise of marriage are somewhat premature. Indeed, she demonstrates that the figures can be interpreted to show marriage in a state of rude health – perhaps not as robust as in the 1950s or 1960s, when it enjoyed exceptional popularity, but nevertheless comparing well with other periods of history. Yet she is intrigued by why some couples have chosen to bypass marriage in their living arrangements. Exploring the question a little further, she draws the conclusion, perhaps surprising for our times, that the economic motive to marry still applies.

Economic rights and entitlements are laid down in law, and the legal contract is the final arbiter in the public domain of whether or not a marriage exists. In Chapter 2, Jane Simpson charts the changing assumptions about the nature of marriage in law by tracking the history of divorce over the past three centuries. Divorce is, perhaps, the most significant change in the family landscape of recent centuries. Why have legal impediments to leaving marriage been removed?

The law contains and reflects public assumptions about the nature of marriage, relationships between men and women and the responsibilities of parenthood. While in a literal sense it is possible to say that divorce is the result of a relaxation in the law, it misses the central point that changes in public attitude are what have made divorce easier. The fundamental shift that has occurred in law is one that has slowly discarded patriarchal and proprietorial assumptions of absolute union in marriage, in which a woman's identity and assets were absorbed by those of her husband, in favour of a more equal recognition of men and women as individuals with responsibilities rather than rights. In other words, the old skin of marriage had, and perhaps still has, to change to accommodate the new wine of egalitarian aspirations in relationships between men and women.

While family law is principally concerned with entitlements to material resources and protecting the interests of children, the Church addresses the moral environment influencing behaviour in marriage. Authority here derives from an historical, scriptural base, which is interpreted to provide a guide for contemporary living. The tie that binds women and men together in this context is more than a contract, and it may be modelled on a religious commitment. Within the Judaeo-Christian tradition, Sue Walrond-Skinner explores in Chapter 3 the covenant between God and the Israelites as a paradigm for the central relationship between women and men in marriage. While the asymmetrical and permanent characteristics of covenant appear to invoke traditional values in marriage, she outlines how they are being reinterpreted today, and considers the symbolic significance of sacrament to the endeavour of making an unconditional commitment in relationships.

At a secular level, psychoanalysis has contributed to our understanding of behaviour in family relationships, and, perhaps, to constructing a value system about these relationships. Unconscious motivation is at the heart of the psychoanalytic preoccupation, and in Chapter 4, Stanley Ruszczynski examines the 'secret contract' of marriage from this perspective. In particular, he examines the connections that people make, quite unconsciously, between their experience of love relationships when growing up and their choice of partner in adult life. An illustration is provided of an unconscious contract in marriage underpinned by a phantasy (spelt in this way to differentiate it from a daydream, or something that is consciously known about) shared by the partners to the effect that the vulnerability of men and the strength of women must remain unacknowledged for either sex to be sustained and not destroyed. Although a phantasy, it powerfully affects behaviour, and Susie Orbach and Sebastian Kraemer examine its workings in a broader context later in the book. Unconscious connections, while being problematic, also

have redemptive possibilities, not least because they offer opportunities to be in touch with oneself and other people. The function of
marriage as a vehicle for development, individually and in relation to
others – of whom the partner is likely to be the most significant other
– takes centre-stage from this perspective.

It is sometimes assumed that psychology has subverted marriage
by emphasizing the pursuit of individual goals to the exclusion of
collective purposes; that it has fostered a narcissism which has
resulted in the 'Me generation'. Yet the particular contribution of
psychoanalysis from its very beginnings has been to attend to the
importance of managing dynamic conflict, both within and between
individuals, and to point out the personal and collective costs when
this is done badly. There is room for hate in love relationships, and
far from advocating divorce for those in conflict, psychoanalysis calls
for the creation of protected space to attend to the meaning of
conflict. Once conflict is legitimized and understood, there is less
compulsion for people to repeat their mistakes with others, or to pass
them on to their children. The question, then, is whether marriage
affords the protected space for partners to talk about, understand,
assimilate and learn from the experiences they generate together.

It is certainly the hope of most couples nowadays that they will be
able to talk to each other, that they will be 'good mates' and that their
relationship will be genuinely companionable. These are more
important qualities for people when selecting their lifetime partner
than social standing, economic position or religious and political
beliefs. But is this necessarily a 'plus' for marriage? A criticism has
been made of psychologically informed counselling and therapeutic
services that, along with media hype, they inflate expectations of
relationships to an unsustainable level. Again, this is to misconstrue
the therapeutic enterprise, which aims in part at creating the
conditions in which people come to recognize the expectations they
bring to their intimate relationships, thereby facilitating the
constructive loss of illusion that is necessary for change. Nevertheless, companionate values can be their own worst enemies in
marriage.

Martin Richards develops this contention in Chapter 5. He traces
the emergence of companionate marriage from its origin in the
middle-class domestic world of the Industrial Revolution, and places
it alongside the parallel rise in divorce during this period. He argues
that it is not the marriage vows that cause problems but our
assumptions about marriage, which contain sufficient contradictions
to explain its current instability. Contradictions between autonomy

and a shared life; between democratic aspirations and the realities of role segregation, particularly once children arrive; between sexual opportunities and monogamous ideals; between what people say and what they do – all these can contribute to a sense of betrayal that is indexed by divorce.

Is it the problem that there are more contradictions and conflicts in marriage nowadays than there used to be, or is it that we manage them differently – perhaps more openly – than before? In Chapter 6, Robert Morley bridges the contributions of Ruszczynski and Richards by examining the interior of two fictional marriages: those of Dorothea and Casaubon in George Eliot's *Middlemarch*, and Irene and Soames in John Galsworthy's *The Forsyte Saga*.

The authors of these accounts were writing in a period spanning the second half of the nineteenth century and the first quarter of the twentieth century, although each set their stories in an earlier time. They therefore provide an interesting contrast to accounts of modern marriage. Or do they? Writing from a psychoanalytical perspective, Morley asserts that many of the elements in contemporary marriage are clearly visible in these accounts of earlier marriage, when the social conditions and moral climate were very different. True, they are fictional accounts, but the classic status of these books attests to their continuing ability to engage us with the predicaments of their characters.

A theme common to both marriages is the struggle to integrate passion into the ordinary business of married life. In both marriages a third party is introduced, whose function it is to articulate the easy sensuality and emotional availability that is missing, and, ultimately, to provide a route to fulfilment for the women. Here again is an echo of the present in the past: women whose expectations of emotional fulfilment in marriage are disappointed by the men they marry. Here, too, is the struggle to preserve fidelity in marriage when the heart is beckoned elsewhere.

Annette Lawson develops this theme in Chapter 7, demonstrating how different things are today in terms of sexual behaviour, and yet how similar in terms of our aspirations towards fidelity. While today men and women are usually sexually experienced before marriage, and while many have sexual relationships outside marriage, fidelity continues to be one of the most highly prized assets of modern marriage. In these circumstances, neither the myth of romantic marriage nor the culture of individualism sustain marriage; instead, they conflict with each other to produce a dissonance that separates belief from behaviour. The sexual behaviour of both sexes has converged, and while this dispels the double standards of Victorian morality, it exposes men and women to the full impact of betrayal when an affair occurs. The ideal of the relationship can be so confounded as to break the marriage, whereas in earlier times it may have constituted less of a crisis – at least for the woman.

Nowadays it is the emotional capital of a relationship that is stolen by an affair, experienced just as keenly by women and men. In days gone by, a woman's infidelity was construed as an offence against the man, something that was of a quite different order to *his* sexual excursions. Adultery was no less than a form of theft, robbing the man of the property of his wife's body and all that might issue from it. Sexual and economic politics were intertwined.

That situation remains, or so argues Mavis Maclean in Chapter 8 as she outlines some economic ties in marriage. Marriage and motherhood combine to depress the earning power and financial entitlements of women and to increase their dependency on men. Here is another situation in which the realities of married life contradict aspirations for marriage to be a partnership of equals. Because she is likely to put his job before her own; because there are likely to be more interruptions to her working life than to his – she carrying the primary responsibility to care first for children and later for ageing relatives – and because we live in a society that accepts serial monogamy while making only limited public provision to cushion its financial consequences, women can find themselves discriminated against in terms in their independent access to economic resources as a result of marriage. The picture may only become evident upon divorce. Opting to cohabit is no safeguard: indeed, cohabiting parents in England and Wales will find themselves less protected in law than their married counterparts in relation to both rights and responsibilities.

The economic imbalance in marriage may prove to be no problem for couples who have few demarcation disputes over the division of labour inside and outside the home, always providing they stay together. As a society we tip the scales in favour of the man working outside the home, while relying on the woman to manage domestic and family responsibilities. If she goes out to work, she will also be expected to retain her household and parental responsibilities; if he cannot go out to work, it will not necessarily be easy for him to assume commensurate responsibilities at home. The only work that is publically recognized and financially rewarded takes place outside the home. Working at home, as well as being bad economics, can undermine self-esteem and unsettle mental health.

So where do men and women belong in this age of equal opportunities? Susie Orbach and Sebastian Kraemer look at both sides of the coin in Chapters 9 and 10 and arrive at similar conclusions. Marriage, for Orbach, is a kind of mental hospital for couples driven mad by trying to keep alive an illusion that men and women occupy the same space, see things in the same way, speak the same language and share the same aspirations in a world that is deeply divided by gender. She argues that the division of labour along lines of gender ensures that the next generation grows up equipped to protect men from owning their need to be looked after and their capacity to care, and women from owning their competence to achieve without compromising their entitlement to be cared for. In consequence, marriage structures the dynamics of dependency in ways that can stifle the development of women and men.

Kraemer traces the rise of patriarchy from Neolithic times to the present day, interweaving the perspectives of social anthropology and psychoanalysis to arrive at an interpretation of what is going on. He argues that the historical rise of patriarchy is a slow version of what happens in the development of each boy in our Western societies. The boy learns that to be a man he must renounce his need of women (principally his mother); join the world of the absent male (his father); and put on a good performance. Haunted and threatened by the power of the archetypal woman, he seeks to gain a hidden proximity to her to restore what he most craves for, while simultaneously maintaining a safe distance by retaining control and subjecting her to envious attacks of one kind or another. This, admittedly, is the negative outcome from child care practices, and it is not a universal feature. What is important is to draw the connections between how we organize our child-rearing and other work commitments today, and the kind of society we are building for tomorrow. Marriage, as *the* institution for cross-gender relationships, is at the centre of negotiations taking place at a private level about the division of labour in society as a whole.

Many of the contributions to this book describe how difficult it is to break the mould of marriage, both individually and institutionally. Our expectations and perceptions are fashioned by blueprints of marriage that we have built up over time, and which, in important respects define our identity. It can then be difficult to recognize the diversity of models that exist in our midst, far less to reconcile them to each other. It is enough of a surprise to discover that one's chosen partner sees things differently. In a multicultural society the differences can be profound and illuminating. Whoever defined marriage as an alliance between just *two* people? Other cultures serve to remind us that this is a nonsense. But how can one think about the differences to shed light on what is going on?

In Chapter 11, Rosine Jozef Perelberg adopts a 'meta' perspective when she draws attention to the 'maps' that guide behaviour and feelings in marriage and family life. These 'maps' are a function of culture, social structure and organization, configured specifically to take account of the different characteristics of individual marriages and how they change over time. They allow for the presence of contradictory meanings, and cut across any tendency to dichotomize what takes place in the privacy of someone's home and what is happening generally in society. The symmetrical 'map', one of the two main types that Perelberg identifies, corresponds with companionate values in marriage, but it should not be assumed to be universal. From her experience in clinical practice she demonstrates how the 'mapping' concept can help people to understand problems that arise in their intimate relationships, and to bring about change.

Where does all this leave marriage? In the final chapter, I suggest that a number of interlocking themes can be helpful in enabling us to understand the nature of contemporary marriage and what is happening to it. Privatization, egalitarianism, the decline of absolute values and the premium placed on individual responsibilities create a number of paradoxes which lie at the heart of marriage today. It is for the couple to make the best of these paradoxes – but not for the couple alone: marriage is an open system; we are all implicated in how it turns out.

There the story ends, at least for the time being. Or, rather, there the stories end. All the chapters in this book are self-sufficient and can be read in any order without reference to other chapters. Equally, all the chapters interlock to form a whole that is both greater than, and forms a backdrop to, its constituent parts. In this it is like marriage itself. And, like marriage, there can be no beginning without an ending, and, of course, no ending without a beginning . . .

Christopher Clulow

1
Whatever Happened to Marriage?

Marriage is always a popular topic, not least because almost everyone has a view on what is or should be happening to it. The view that I shall be taking in this chapter is the 'macro' perspective. My understanding of what goes on in British marriages is informed by demographic and statistical information and by a sociological understanding, as well as knowledge of social policy and historical dimensions of family life.

Historically, marriage and families are constantly being discussed as if they were in a state of crisis. Sociologists are interested in why this is so. Gittins (1985) points out that this phenomenon is not new, and

> . . . causes most concern during periods of economic recession, when there is change in the rate of population growth, and/or during times when fear of political unrest and upheaval is acute. The three often go together and provide an insight into why the family becomes a political issue during such periods . . . so when concern about a crisis in the family becomes a recurrent theme what is probably being expressed is a fear that *society itself* is in a state of crisis. (p.55)

My task is not to moralize about marriage or to focus on the very outlandish – which is often how public or political discussion treats the issue – but to look at some of the evidence, as far as we have evidence, about what the trends are, and then to discuss and explain what they might mean. The emphasis will be more on describing than explaining.

The Popularity of Marriage

Popular discussion about marriage is frequently cavalier about the statistics it uses. It is said that marriage is declining, and that the traditional family of a married couple with dependent children is now a minority of the population. However, we need to distinguish between households and people as the unit of analysis. While the

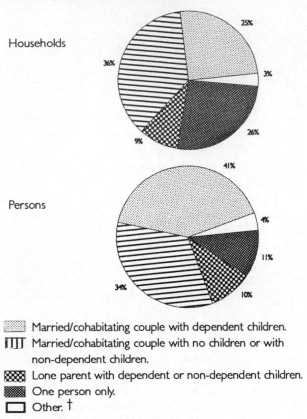

Households

Persons

Married/cohabitating couple with dependent children.

Married/cohabitating couple with no children or with non-dependent children.

Lone parent with dependent or non-dependent children.

One person only.

Other. †

*Households categorized by the type of family they contain. In the lone-parent and married couple households, other individuals who were not family member may also have been present.

† 'Other' includes households containing two or more unrelated adults and those containing two or more families.

Source: GHS 1991 (OPCS Monitor SS92/1).
From IYF Factsheet 1 - 'Putting families on the map'.

Figure 1: British households and people by type of household in 1991.

'traditional' married, or living as married, couple with children comprised 25 per cent of households in Great Britain in 1991 compared with 31 per cent in 1971, they constituted 41 per cent of people in 1991 (see Figure 1).

Moreover, if we add the 34 per cent of people who are married with no dependent children – which will include those who intend to have children, and those whose children are no longer dependent, as well as the permanently childless – then three-quarters of adults in 1991 were currently married or cohabiting, most of whom have or will have children. And if we adopt a lifetime view, we might well include those currently in the single category either because they are young and will marry eventually, or because they are widowed. Adding these together, we can see that the vast majority of people will marry at least once in their lifetime.

This lifetime perspective illustrates one of the problems we have when we talk about the nature of people's family relationships, their experiences and the type of family they live in: all our statistics and most research evidence is cross-sectional; so, like a snapshot, they represent only one point in time. Increasingly, those of us interested in family change and family diversity are arguing that we need to know about all the different lifetime family experiences people have. It is not enough to understand what is happening to families and marriage from the snapshot perspective. We need to know very much more about people's lifetime movements across different family situations.

Classically, people are born into their family or household of origin, and this is likely to be headed by a married couple. They may move away and live independently – either on their own or with a group of students or friends – before living in their family of creation with a partner and probably their own children. This arrangement ends when adult children move away and one of the partners dies. Most people, even in this very simple model, experience a variety of family or household situations over their lifetime. Clearly there will be many complex variations depending on whether people have one or more marriages; periods of living alone or cohabiting; or living with stepchildren or step parents, and so on.

The difficulty is that it is impossible to get a sense of the reality of people's lifetime family and marital experiences because of the restricted way in which the information has been collected. However, an historical perspective offers an important insight. The 1950s and 1960s are often looked upon as the golden era of marriage and family relationships, against which subsequent decades are compared unfavourably. Yet as Graph 1 shows, the proportion of people who are married at any one point in time has fluctuated over the last century. Indeed, it might be argued that it is the marked rise in the proportion of the adult population in England and Wales (not Great Britain on this occasion) who were married in the 1950s, 1960s and 1970s which may be the deviation rather than the patterns of subsequent decades.

There are all sorts of reasons for these changes, partly related to the demographic structure of the population as well as the propensity to marry, but the key thing to remember is that historically marriage rates have varied. The reasons for this are complex, and lower rates do not necessarily mean the institution is in decline.

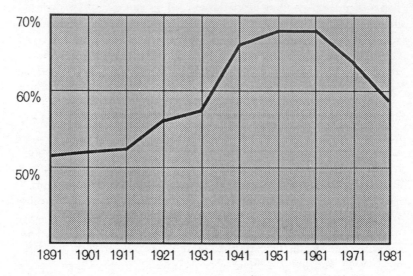

Source: GHS 1991 (OPCS Monitor SS92/1).
From IYF Factsheet 1 - 'Putting families on the map'.

Graph 1: Married population as a percentage of all adult population in England and Wales from 1891 to 1991.

However, in the late 1980s there was growing public concern in Britain about the apparent rise in marital and family breakdown. As political pronouncements, which reached a crescendo in the autumn of 1993, showed, this has overwhelmingly focused on the decline of households containing married couples with children and the consequent growth of lone-parent households, the vast majority of which are headed by a mother. Two elements in this development caused political concern. First, as parents separated and divorced, the father's material and emotional roles in supporting his children diminished; increasingly, the financial aspect of his role was being taken on by the state. Second, the growth in single, never-married mothers suggested there had been a flight from marriage: mothers were willing to reject men, and men were prepared to abandon the role of husband and father; both expected the state to take on the still necessary role of financial provider.

Table 1 shows the changes that occurred over the 20 year period from 1971 to 1991. Whereas over nine out of ten families with dependent children were headed by a married or cohabitating couple in 1971 (and very few of these would have been cohabiting), there was a steady drop in this to just about eight out of ten in 1991. The large growth in lone-parent families, to just under one in five of all families with dependent children, has been accounted for by both an increase in divorced and separated mothers, and also a rise in single mothers who have never married. The proportion of lone fathers, who comprise about one in ten of all lone parents, has remained relatively steady over the period.

What these statistics cannot tell us is whether the single never married-mother category in 1991 contained the same sort of mother as in 1971. All the evidence suggests that it does not: the 1991 category is likely to comprise mothers whose cohabiting relationships have broken down, as well as the more 'traditional' single mother. Many of these mothers would have been more likely to have married in the 1970s, although they may still have eventually

Table 1: Families with dependent children* Great Britain

	1971	1981	1991
	%	%	%
Married/cohabiting couple	92	87	81
Lone mother	7	11	18
single	1	2	6
widowed	2	2	1
divorced	2	4	6
separated	2	2	4
Lone father	1	2	1
All lone parents	8	13	19
Base = 100%	4864	4445	3143

* Dependent children are under 16, or aged 16–18 and in full-time education, in the family unit and living in the household.

Source GHS 1991 (OPCS Monitor SS92/1).

entered the lone-mother category as separated or divorced mothers after the breakdown of early or teenage marriages.

European Comparisons

How does the UK compare in marriage and divorce rates with other countries in the European Union? Here we have the rather paradoxical situation of the UK having the second highest marriage rate in the Union after Portugal, and the second highest divorce rate after Denmark. Comparisons need to be made with care, however,

Table 2: Marriage and divorce – EC comparison, 1981 and 1990

	Marriages per 1,000 eligible population		Divorces per 1,000 existing marriages	
	1981	1990	1981	1990
UK[1]	7.1	6.8	11.9	12.6
Belgium	6.5	6.5	6.1	8.7
Denmark	5.0	6.1	12.1	12.8
France[2]	5.8	5.1	6.8	8.4
Germany (Fed. Rep.)	5.8	6.6	7.2	8.1
Greece	7.3	5.8	2.5	
Irish Republic	6.0	5.0	0.0	0.0
Italy	5.6	5.4	0.9	2.9
Luxembourg[2]	5.5	6.1	5.9	10.0
Netherlands	6.0	6.4	8.3	8.1
Portugal	7.7	7.3	2.8	
Spain	5.4	5.5	1.1	
Eur 12	6.0	6.0		

[1] 1990 column for marriages contains 1989 data, and divorce column contains 1987 data.
[2] 1990 column for divorces contains 1989 data.

Source: Statistical Office of the European Communities. From Social Trends 23, 1993, HMSO.

because like is not necessarily being compared with like. For example, Portugal may have the highest marriage rate in the European Union, but it has a very different socio-economic structure; the rate may change as Portugal becomes more industrialized.

Table 2 shows that the UK has had a slight drop in marriage rate, which has been confirmed by more recent statistics; although it is high, there is a slight downward trend. This is true of the majority of European countries. When we combine the figures in the table with those for the 1970s, it is clear that marriage rates have fallen quite dramatically in Europe overall. Marriages peaked in 1972 at 3.7 million, and they have fallen since then by about 20 per cent. This has been caused in part by a postponement of marriage, and in part by a rejection of it. Rejection seems to have been higher in the Scandinavian countries, which are often seen as pointing the way for other European countries, although there is no simple association.

Differences of culture, religion and socio-economic structures also underlie the different divorce rates across the European Union. However, there are some common trends in both marriage and divorce rates. With the exception of the Irish Republic, where divorce is unavailable, almost all the countries in the European Union have experienced an increase in divorce. During the 1980s they have also experienced a rise of between two to four years in the age at which people marry for the first time, with countries like Denmark having the highest average age, followed by Germany, the Netherlands and then the UK, France and Luxembourg (Dormor, 1992).

However, while a minority of individual marriages may be breaking down, and while the institution itself is under some pressure and may be less popular with the young, marriage is still popular enough for people to try it more than once. A striking feature of the current marriage figures is the proportion of all marriages which are remarriages. In 1971, 20 per cent of all marriages in the UK were remarriages for one or both partners; by 1990 remarriages accounted for 36 per cent of all marriages, of which 16 per cent were second or subsequent marriages for both partners (Central Statistical Office, 1993).

The Growth in Cohabitation

Developments in marriage have to be looked at in the context of the growth in cohabitation – couples living together (according to the General Household Survey for six months or more) without being married. Popular thinking sees this as a phenomenon of the 1980s and 1990s, and often grossly overstates current levels of cohabitation. Cohabitation has always existed, particularly before legal marriage became widely accepted during the nineteenth century, or when divorce was not available to deal with marriage breakdown.

What is new is the increase in cohabitation over the last 20 years, in particular the increase in 'nubile cohabitation', that is, where people in their 20s and 30s live together either as a prelude or an alternative to marriage. A measure of the recent nature of this interest is that we have only had national statistics on cohabitation since the 1979 General Household Survey. In 1991, just over five per cent of adults in Britain were cohabitating. The peak ages for cohabiting are 20 to 24 for women and 25 to 34 for men. At any one time, just over ten per cent of the under 35s were cohabiting in 1991, compared with 2.5 per cent of people over 35. Overall, about two-thirds of cohabitants are under 35 (Kiernan and Estaugh, 1993).

This rise in cohabitation is a wide-spread phenomenon. While Scandinavia may appear to be leading the way – with about 13 per cent in Sweden and 16 per cent in Denmark of adults cohabiting – countries like France (10 per cent), the Netherlands (7 per cent), and Belgium (7 per cent) had higher rates than the UK in 1990 (Dormor 1992). For all these countries, cohabitation is chiefly a practice of the young. About 31 per cent of Swedish women aged 20 to 24, and 37 per cent of similarly aged Danish women were in a cohabiting relationship in 1990, compared with 15 per cent of British women of the same age, and 19 per cent of young French women.

As usual, a snapshot picture underplays the extent to which cohabiting has become a majority, if transient, experience. Among women marrying for the first time between 1985 and 1988, 58 per cent had cohabited with their future husband. This compares with 33 per cent of those marrying during 1975 to 1979, and 6 per cent of those marrying in the late 1960s (Kiernan and Estaugh, 1993). The rapid growth in nubile cohabitation is shown very clearly in Graph 2.

Cohabiting unions tend to be short-term and child-free. They last about two years on average, and either convert into marriage or break up. As yet, few have lasted for long periods, although it is hard to know if this is beginning to change and what proportion might replace marriage permanently. The dramatic increase in the proportion of those cohabiting – a doubling over the 1980s – suggests that it will be increasingly necessary to distinguish between different types of cohabitants as a starting point for understanding the changes taking place. Kiernan and Estaugh drew such distinctions in their

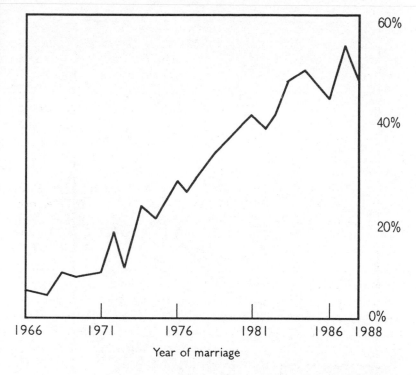

Source: Office of Population Censuses and Surveys,
from Social Trends 22,1992, HMSO.

Graph 2: Proportion of women who cohabited with their future
husband before marriage (by year of marriage).

analysis of cohabitants recorded in the 1989 General Household
Survey. Distinguishing initially between single, never-married and
post-marital cohabitants, they subsequently identified a third group:
never-married couples with children. About one in six cohabitants
were in this group, compared with one in two in the young and
child-free group, or one in three in the post-marital group. These
groups were compared on a range of simple socio-economic
variables. Few differences were found between childless married and
cohabiting couples. However, there were marked differences
between married and cohabiting couples who had had children. On
most measures, cohabiting couples with children were less well off
than their married counterparts.

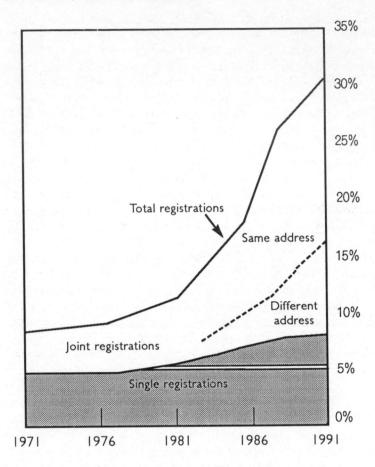

Source: Office of Population Censuses and Surveys

Graph 3: Live births outside marriage as a percentage of all births by registration in England and Wales.

The Rise in Extramarital Births

The dramatic rise in the number of babies born outside marriage has excited considerable public comment. While seven out of ten births still take place inside marriage, the major feature of the 1980s has been the separation of marriage and child-bearing for a significant minority of the child-bearing population. At the turn of the century, between four and five per cent of babies were born outside marriage. With the exception of the war years, this remained the picture until

1960. It rose to 11 per cent in 1979 and then started to climb steeply so that by 1991 about 30 per cent of all births in the UK took place outside marriage. There are some local differences. For example, the proportion is lower in Northern Ireland, at 20 per cent.

There is a link between cohabitation and the rise in extramarital births. As Graph 3 shows, the proportion of babies jointly registered by their unmarried parents has increased from 46 per cent in 1971 to 75 per cent in 1991, and half of these are registered at the same address. This suggests that some 50 per cent of babies born outside marriage are born to a cohabiting couple. These administrative statistics tell us nothing about the nature of these relationships, for example, the extent to which parents not living together are doing this through choice because of the workings of the benefit system, or as a result of difficulties in finding adequate housing. To unpack this we need special studies.

It is useful to see how the UK compares with other European countries. There has been a noticeable increase in child-bearing outside marriage in many northern and western European countries. The Scandinavians have the highest proportion, with 50 per cent of babies being born outside marriage in Sweden (and Iceland); 46 per cent in Denmark, and 39 per cent in Norway. The UK is also quite high on the list, along with France, Austria and Finland. Between a quarter to one-third of babies are born outside marriage in these countries. By contrast, extramarital births are relatively low in West Germany, the Netherlands, Italy and Switzerland (11 per cent or less in 1989), and lowest of all in Greece (2 per cent). This suggests that while marriage is increasingly losing its monopoly on partnerships in these countries, this does not necessarily constitute a rejection of marriage outright: couples frequently marry at later ages, often after the birth of a first or second child. Even where cohabitation has been long standing, as in Sweden and Denmark, the majority of women in unions in their 30s are married.

Longterm Cohabiting Mothers

If more parents are eschewing marriage, it is important to understand why this is happening. I want now to look at what we know about a statistically rare group of people – mothers who cohabit longterm – and to consider to what extent they have rejected marriage, and why.

Two recent studies throw light on these issues. In their analysis of the characteristics of cohabitants, Kiernan and Estaugh (1993) compare married and cohabiting couples with children on some basic socio-economic measures. As Table 3 shows, cohabiting couples on average have significantly lower household incomes; are more likely than married couple families to be in receipt of income support and housing benefit, and to be in local authority accommodation; and the male partner is more likely to be unemployed or in semi-skilled and unskilled occupations.

Table 3: Married and Cohabiting Couples

	Couples with children	
	Cohabiting	Married
% incomes under £100	23	6
% local authority housing	50	20
% receiving housing benefit	26	10
% no qualifications	43	25
% unemployed male	19	4
% in semi-skilled and unskilled occupations	46	18

Source: 1989 General Household Survey; from Kiernan and Estaugh (1993)

In her study of longterm cohabiting mothers, McRae (1993) also found that a large majority lived in 'disadvantaged circumstances'; one implication of her study is that this group has less material interest to protect and therefore less need to marry. Indeed, her study showed that among longterm cohabiting mothers 'those with most assets to bequeath married soonest.'

McRae's study focused on the critical issue of why 'increasing numbers of women were remaining unmarried after having children'. Two aspects of the study are particularly illuminating. First, she documents the steady flow of cohabiting mothers into marriage. Over a four-year period between the first and second interview, a sizeable minority had married, and more expected to do so some day. McRae argues that the actual number who had subsequently married was an artefact of her interview timetable. An earlier or later interview would have led to fewer or more being married than her study showed.

Second, she examines the reasons women gave for both marrying and not marrying, as well as the reported advantages and disadvantages of cohabitation. This presents a complex picture of the competing internal and external pressures on women in this situation. Outside influences played some part, but few reported direct societal or family pressure. A minority of women who married after having a baby in a cohabiting relationship reported parental pressure. More usually, however, any pressure was internal, and concerned with the need for security either for the mother herself or, more usually, for her children. Marriage was also seen as a way of making a commitment to the relationship.

Women who were still cohabiting were less deciding not to marry than taking no decision as such: '. . . You don't sit down and first say "we're not getting married" ', said one mother. McRae found that this was part of a more general apathy about marriage where the mothers in her sample could see no advantage in getting married: 'I've just got no interest in being married. We live as a couple and we are quite satisfied with the way we are. I've been married and it's no different from living together.'

Rather surprisingly, perhaps, the cost of weddings were given as a reason for not getting married by about one-quarter of the women. Clearly the 'big day' element of weddings meant that some of these women would rather wait until they could do it properly, while others associated marriage with 'so much wasted money'. Other reasons for not marrying were more negative about the institution. About 30 per cent cited the fear of divorce as a reason for not marrying: 'Everyone in my family that has been married is divorced. I don't think it's worth getting married. To me it's a lot of pain getting married and breaking up.' Only a small minority (21 per cent), however, were opposed to marriage on ideological grounds, saying they disliked the institution of marriage for such reasons as, 'I find it oppressive.'

In concluding her study, McRae does not necessarily see parental cohabitation as a threat to marriage. For some people it, like child-free or nubile cohabitation, is a transient phase; parents go on to marry eventually. And she suggests the internal dynamics of long term cohabiting relationships are not so markedly different from married relationships.

Her study was not designed to throw light on whether cohabiting families are more stable than married families. This would require larger studies that tracked people over time. National data suggest a greater chance of relationship breakdown in cohabiting than married couples (Haskey 1992) although there are all sorts of caveats that have to be added to this. It really is too early to tell whether the sort of longterm cohabiting unions we are beginning to see, and which McRae's study highlights, will be as stable as married unions or will replace them. What we can say is that it is still very atypical to have children in a longterm, non-married relationship, and that most people who do so are living in disadvantaged circumstances. The small group of affluent, highly educated women in this position are truly exceptional; their experiences are currently far from the norm.

Attitudes to Marriage

What, then, are the more general attitudes to marriage, cohabitation and extramarital child-bearing? We have both European and British attitudinal studies which throw some light on this. The European Values Study, undertaken in 1990, shows that marriage is far from an outdated institution for the vast majority of Europeans (Ashford and Timms, 1992). Surprisingly, more French, Portuguese, Belgian and Dutch respondents (about one in five) felt the institution was outdated than Swedish or Norwegian respondents (just over one in ten). About 17 per cent of the UK sample thought marriage was out of date. There were also important variations in attitudes by age. Older people were more likely than younger people to be supportive of marriage as an institution, and less likely to recommend cohabitation. They were also more likely to feel that 'people who want children should get married'.

**Table 4: Marriage is an Outdated Institution:
Do You Agree or Disagree?**

	Yes	No	Don't know
France	27	66	7
Portugal	22	74	4
Belgium	20	71	9
Netherlands	20	76	4
Great Britain	17	81	2
Denmark	17	78	5
N. Ireland	14	84	2
Italy	13	82	5
Spain	13	82	6
Sweden	13	81	6
W. Germany	12	72	15
Ireland	10	89	2
Norway	10	86	5

Source: European Values Study 1990

Kiernan and Estaugh show similar results in their analysis of British attitudes to cohabitation and births out of marriage. While very few people of any age would advise young people to cohabit rather than marry, there was majority support from younger age groups for pre-marital cohabitation. Moreover, a majority (57 per cent) of under-24s did not agree with the proposition that people

Table 5: Advice Would Give To a Young Person

Age	Cohabit before marriage %	Cohabit only %	Total %
18–24 years	59	9	68
25–34	58	5	63
35–44	55	7	62
45–54	37	3	40
55–59	25	0	25
60–64	29	1	30
65 or older	19	1	20

Source: British Social Attitudes Survey, 1989; from Kiernan and Estaugh, 1993.

Table 6: Percentage agreeing with the proposition that 'People who want children ought to get married.'

Age	%	N
18–24 years	43	167
25–34	51	254
35–44	65	248
45–54	80	207
55–59	89	91
60–64	91	89
65 or older	92	248
No answer	–	3
Total	70	1307

Source: British Social Attitudes Survey, 1989; from Kiernan and Estaugh, 1993.

wanting children ought to marry. What is hard to know is whether these differences are age-related, and whether younger people will change their minds as they grow older and adopt more traditional attitudes. I suspect there will be some ageing effect, but that we are also seeing cohort differences which will be sustained.

There is no doubt that the institution of marriage appears to be under threat, but perhaps the threat is more apparent than real. It is still true that the vast majority of adults will marry, and a majority of them will marry only once, with their relationship being ended by the death of their partner. However, there is an air of uncertainty about marriage which is in part engendered by public awareness of marital breakdown and the apparent rejection of marriage by young people. It is also in part engendered by the changing dynamics of the married relationship and different – some might say rising – expectations that couples, and particularly women in partnerships, have of marriage.

I want to suggest that we need to take a measured view on marriage and not be pressured into feeling that the changes are all negative. We should also ensure that we take a structural perspective and ask why these changes are happening. Remembering C. Wright Mills's (1959) phrase 'private troubles, public issues', we should be spending less time criticizing or condemning groups of individuals for their changed behaviour and more time trying to understand what is happening. In particular, we need to ask what are the societal pressures, strains and stresses currently placed on marriage and family relations. The tendency to blame individuals for their own difficulties often overrides discussion about whether social institutions structured in one era need to be remade to meet the conditions of another. The question is: what do we want to preserve from our former conceptions of marriage, and how can we as members of society construct appropriate frameworks so that people can sustain the sort of relationships they want as individuals, as members of couples and families which society requires if the emotional and social needs of adults and children are to be adequately met?

Ceridwen Roberts

2
The Changing Legal Context

In 1809, the Archbishop of Canterbury lamented at the

> ... pollution of divorce bills now daily more frequent, so common indeed were they, that ... they seemed to be considered as the proper fruits of marriage ... It was impossible that such things could last long. (Wolfram, 1987, p.147)

The sentiment is perhaps in line with current opinion, but with the difference that divorce in 1809 was occurring at the alarming rate of three per year, compared with 170,000 in the UK today.

Divorce and separation have now largely replaced death as disruptors of the early and middle years of marriage. Nearly two out of five contemporary marriages founder before their 25th anniversary, and one in five children will experience the divorce of their parents by the age of 16.

The most obvious practical change in English kinship over the past two to three centuries has therefore been the introduction and increasing prevalence of divorce. Since the removal of legal impediment is often blamed for the increase in divorce, the question arises as to why it should have been forbidden in England for centuries and then made progressively easier to obtain? I shall address this question by summarizing some of the legal changes which have affected the marriage contract itself and the assumptions they contain about marriage.

Marriage as Merger

The institution of marriage is the legally sanctioned union of one man with one woman. In England, marriage is very simple and inexpensive to contract. It requires three weeks notice or a licence and a brief, theoretically public, ceremony (either religious, or, since 1836, civil) and the signing of a register. This must be followed by 'consummation', that is, an act of sexual intercourse.

Thus has the bargain been struck for centuries. On the surface, a simple mutual agreement for lifelong cohabitation. But what were the inferred terms of the contract? From the man's point of view, the deal seemed advantageous: the wife, in effect, signed herself over to him. This followed the Christian view of marriage of the husband and wife being 'as one', and 'of one flesh'. Under the Common Law a married woman had no legal identity apart from her husband. The wife thus became 'part' of the husband, taking his name, rank, status and domicile. Property and custody over children were vested in him, as was liability for debts. Neither could give evidence against the other, nor could they form a conspiracy. Sexual intercourse was to be confined to husband and wife. It was, in theory, an absolute union, to be broken only by death.

From the woman's perspective, the bargain seemed poor. Although the two were called 'one person in law' for the purpose of inferring that whatever was hers was his, the parallel inference – that whatever was his was hers – was never drawn. The wife's existence was simply regarded as having merged into that of her husband. This was the position until 1870.

Furthermore, she was required to satisfy any physical demands her husband might make on the basis of having consented through marriage to sexual intercourse on demand with her husband once and for all. It was only in 1991 that the Law Lords overruled Chief Justice Hale's dictum of 1736 that there was no such offence as marital rape. This injustice, by today's standard, was compounded by the fact that dual standards of sexual behaviour were prevalent: the requirement of sexual fidelity was applied more stringently to the wife than to her husband. Because she was seen as the property of her husband, adultery was regarded as theft. In parliamentary debates as late as the mid-nineteenth century it was said that '. . . it was possible for a wife to pardon a husband who had committed adultery; but it was hardly possible for a husband ever really to pardon the adultery of a wife.' (Wolfram, 1987, p.87) One might wonder whether some things never really change!

Whatever induced the woman into such a contract? Well, marriage provided her with respectability, rank, sometimes wealth, and, of course, the only means for a God-fearing woman to produce offspring. In other words, marriage provided the way for women to fulfil their traditional and expected role in society.

These time-honoured and binding terms of the contract envisaged no break clause. So when did the unthinkable begin?

Divorce: the Beginning

Divorce did not exist in any form in England until around 1700. Before the Reformation the Catholic Church forbade it, although it accepted grounds on which marriages could be annulled and apparent marriages declared to have been no marriage. After the Reformation there was provision for divorce in most Protestant countries of Europe, including Scotland, interestingly enough, which introduced it for adultery or malicious desertion by either sex.

England stood out as the exception. The Church of England was as steadfast as the Catholics in refusing to countenance divorce. Therein, perhaps, lies a fundamental key to the slow progress of divorce law in England – the implacable hostility of the Church of England. To claim that something accorded with the Scriptures or went against God's word could be used to justify the *status quo*. The Hardwicke Marriage Act of 1753 confirmed the monopoly of the Established Church over weddings, and it was determined to retain control over the institution of marriage. The divorce question was therefore to become embroiled in the wider battle between Church and State, religion and secularism. As the powers of the Church ebbed, and the part it played in everyday life diminished, so did its ability to halt the progress of divorce.

Ironically, the Church did have a hand in easing legal separation after the Reformation. The ecclesiastical courts granted divorce *a mensa et thoro* (from board and bed) for adultery and cruelty. This was available to both sexes. It was not divorce as we understand it because it did not permit remarriage; this would have transgressed the statutes against bigamy. These 'divorces' may therefore more accurately be termed what were later to become known as judicial separations. They were, none the less, an important precedent for the real thing.

The ecclesiastical courts also granted another form of divorce *a vinculo matrimonii* (from the bonds of marriage). This allowed remarriage, but it was again not divorce in the sense that we understand it today since it was only granted if the original marriage could be declared invalid. By the nineteenth century these were being referred to as annulments, usually on the grounds of lack of consent or non-consummation.

To contract an invalid marriage was not illegal; to go through a marriage with an undissolved marriage on your hands most definitely was. In the face of penalties that included death or transportation, divorce was unsurprisingly slow to arrive in a fashion that permitted remarriage while the former spouse was still alive.

Private Acts of Parliament

The first dissolution of marriage generally considered to have been a genuine divorce – that is, a valid marriage being dissolved to permit remarriage – was the case of Lord Roos in 1670. This was obtained by private Act of Parliament on the ground of his wife's adultery. Lord Roos must have been a determined man indeed, since the process took eight years to effect. He had been helped by royal support from Charles II, a not altogether disinterested supporter, who was hoping to rid himself of his own wife and find another to produce a legitimate male heir to the throne.

This Act set a trend. The Earl of Macclesfield obtained a divorce in 1698 and the Duke of Norfolk, after nine years of trying, in 1700. Parliament then decided that the dissolution of marriage to enable remarriage came within its jurisdiction. This may, perhaps, have been in no small measure because cases were heard in glorious detail by the House of Lords and then referred to the House of Commons. The details of Lady Roos attempting to titillate the Lord by dressing up as a boy might well have prevented their learned Lordships from dozing off in a way that some modern debates do not! Indeed, Charles II attended Parliament in disguise and declared he found Lady Roos' sexual exploits 'better than a play'. (Wolfram, 1987, p.78)

The process was, however, costly and time consuming. Applicants needed already to have secured a divorce *a mensa et thoro* for adultery from the ecclesiastical court, and by the end of the eighteenth century the petitioner also needed to have pursued a successful case for damages against the wife's lover for 'criminal conversation' at the King's Bench or other secular court (although women petitioners were excluded from the need to claim against the mistress). Damages could be as high as £20,000 in addition to the husband's costs.

Between 1700 and 1750 there were 14 divorces, and between 1750 and 1800 there were 117 cases. However, it was only in 1801 that the first successful case was brought by a woman, and there were only four such divorces secured by private Act of Parliament. Adultery was the ground for divorce, but women had the harder task of having to prove this in conjunction with incest or bigamy.

Blame and fault were the crucial elements of divorce. In 1711 one Sarah Bell was described in an Act as 'a woman of bad fame and lewd conversation', and an even more unfortunate Mrs Cobb as 'a Common Prostitute, Night-Walker and a Notorious Thief', and furthermore 'the wickedest woman in the world!' (Wolfram, 1987, p.80) How Mr Cobb discharged the burden of proof as to the latter allegation is not recorded.

The Matrimonial Causes Act 1857

Divorce, although becoming more common by 1850, still remained a prerogative of the upper classes, even though the occasional aggrieved butcher and farmer managed to have his day in Parliament. Yet as England progressed into the nineteenth century a great tide of reform was gathering. 1792 had seen the French introduce legalized divorce on the grounds of mutual incompatibility. In England, political privilege was being extended down through the social system to the ranks of the middling sort. The remark by Professor Daniel Bell that 'what the few have today, the many will demand tomorrow' could be well applied to the issue of access to divorce. In the mid-1800s, a political platform of extending to the poorer classes what the upper classes already had was a popular one.

Furthermore, the secularization of marriage itself was underway. Marriage in register offices was introduced in 1836, and within 20 years accounted for five per cent of all marriages. Courts were awarding lower damages for adultery, perhaps reflecting that divorce had become a more recognized part of the social scene and the reality that adulterers often absconded, making damages hard to collect. Secular power was growing, and the Church was a popular target. The ecclesiastical courts were exposed as corrupt and inefficient by a Commission in 1824. The Bishops, even from their privileged benches in the House of Lords, could no longer dictate policy. Moreover, a hop over the border into Scotland could secure a cheap divorce, although no return to England was possible. In 1850 a Royal Commission was set up to study divorce, headed, perhaps significantly, by a Scot, Lord Campbell. This heralded legislative change.

The Matrimonial Causes Act of 1857 was promoted as a *procedural* change rather than anything greater, bringing England into line with the simpler, less-expensive process in Scotland, and transforming divorce into a *judicial* process. Reformers liked to quote Lord Maule's judgement in a case of bigamy in 1845, which mapped out the current procedures. The culprit, who pleaded that he had remarried without obtaining a divorce because he could not afford a divorce, was castigated for not having spent the necessary £1,000, which he did not possess. Maule lingered with loving detail on the procedures he would have had to go through to obtain a divorce, and pronounced as his sentence for bigamy one day's imprisonment, already served.

The Act was never intended as the first significant change in English divorce law since the sixteenth century that it became, but it was hijacked and widened by reformers, and pushed through by Prime Minister Palmerston, who kept Parliament in session during the hottest summer in living memory. The result of the Act was to abolish criminal conversation cases, ecclesiastical and parliamentary divorce. Divorces *a mensa et thoro* became judicial separation, private Acts were replaced by judicial divorces and all was administered by a single court.

The increase in the divorce rate was steady but not spectacular. By 1900 there were around 500 divorces a year in a married population of 11 million. Although 1857 stands out as a watershed in divorce reform, it marks only the end of the beginning of the story of divorce.

Unshackling Women

The key to further divorce reform, and perhaps the increase in divorce, may lie in the movement towards women's emancipation. As has been seen, the marriage contract was restrictive for women, and there grew a tide of opposition to the dominance of patriarchy, which for centuries had reduced women to the nearest approximation of a slave. Abandoned or separated wives could not even resist their profligate husbands coming back and claiming their property long after separation.

The 1857 Act extended a woman's grounds for divorce, but only to allow divorce for adultery compounded by desertion, whereas the man only had to prove adultery. During the parliamentary debates, Lord Chancellor Cranworth declared it harsh to punish a husband who was merely 'a little profligate', whereas for a woman to be divorced for adultery was still to render her a social outcast. In easing the grounds for men to petition, and refusing women the right to be treated in the same way, the Bill was actually *opposed* by women, supported by Gladstone who feared the measure would lead to the 'degradation of women'. It took until 1923 for the grounds for divorce to be placed on an equal footing between women and men.

Perhaps a more important step for women was the gaining of rights over property. *The Subjection of Women*, published in 1869, included an article entitled 'The Property Disabilities of a Married

Woman, and Other Legal Effects of Marriage'. This, among other factors, acted as a catalyst for the campaign for property rights for women and culminated in the Married Women's Property Acts of 1870 and the early 1880s. The earnings of a woman, and any property she brought into the marriage or acquired during it, were now her own. Married women could dispose of property by will or otherwise, sue or be sued, and carry out separate trades or businesses. They became liable for debts contracted before marriage, and for maintaining spouses and dependants in the same way as married men. Husbands and wives could also institute civil and criminal proceedings against each other with respect to property.

The Married Women's Property Acts were hailed as a milestone in the emancipation of women. By recognizing a wife's separate economic existence within marriage, a nail was hammered into the coffin of the idea of the union of husband and wife. No longer could it be said that they were one person and that person was the husband. In practice, the general trend was towards allowing 'equity' to prevail in property disputes rather than the husband's rights. For a time, the division of property between a husband and wife in the event of divorce followed legal ownership. However, when the Matrimonial Proceedings and Property Act of 1970 came into force the principle was established that in divorce the matrimonial property or family assets were to be aggregated and then fairly divided between the parties. This concept of 'equitable distribution' continues to underlie our current law.

It is worth adding that the way in which courts interpret equitable distribution favours women in some respects today. Given the same facts, but in one case the man having the bulk of the assets and earnings and in the other the wife having them, a judge is likely to make a higher order against the husband than the wife.

In addition to property rights, the education and political enfranchisement of women were further nails in the coffin of marriage as a patriarchal union. The 1850s saw the foundation of girls' schools and of Bedford Women's College at the University of London. This was followed by the introduction of compulsory general education in the 1870s. It was not long before women were demanding a right to vote, something that was achieved in 1869 for single women in municipal elections. By some strange dint of logic, married women were not given this right until 1894. Perhaps it was assumed that they would automatically vote as their husbands did! Be that as it may, the campaign, that would achieve full electoral emancipation for women in 1918 was well underway.

Women have also gained legal rights over children. Children had been regarded as the property of fathers, entirely at their disposal and subject to their control. Fathers were legally empowered to remove children, put them to work, and marry them off without consulting their spouses, who usually carried the chief responsibilities for rearing them.

The Infant Custody Act of 1839 was the first step towards removing some of these inequalities. Gradually, the responsibility of child-rearing was recognized as being jointly held between the parents. More recently still, the emphasis has come to be on 'responsibility' towards children rather than on 'rights and duties' enshrined in the old law. The interests and welfare of children became the paramount consideration for courts, and residence with the mother the most usual parenting arrangement after divorce. Whether this will change as fathers become more involved in practical childcare remains an open question.

The present situation rests on the concept of joint parenting built into the Children Act of 1989, which stressed the child's rights and welfare as the paramount consideration for the judiciary. Law reform has also removed the legal disabilities of illegitimate children, and increased the rights of mothers to claim support from fathers, most recently by the Child Support Act of 1991. The recognition of parents by the law no longer depends on marital status.

No one can read the history of marriage, even in our own time, without being struck both by the material inequalities suffered by earlier generations of wives and how these have reduced in recent decades. As the role of women in society has altered beyond recognition, so the rules within the marriage contract have had to accommodate these changes. In this way the emancipation of women may be seen as going hand in hand with changes in divorce law.

The Movement Away From Fault

Even after the 1857 Act, the pillar of divorce law remained the matrimonal offence. That adultery was for so long the only offence for which divorce was possible may be evidence of the importance attached to sexual faithfulness in marriage in England, especially in relation to women. However, by the late nineteenth century, adultery by women had become a very much less heinous offence than before, to judge by the content of plays on the London stage in the 1890s. Legislation progressively added grounds for which 'relief' might be sought.

As divorce became more prevalent, and divorce petitions were increasingly undefended, there was a movement away from fault and blame in procedures. Society was less easily scandalized. Proof of adultery became a mockery of the system, and connivance and collusion abounded. As the *Encyclopedia Britannica* of 1929 recorded, one result of equalizing the grounds of divorce between the sexes was the marked increase in the number of wives' suits in which the charge was based on a solitary incident in a hotel. The husband would 'act the gentleman' and spend a weekend in a hotel with a hired person, placing his shoes outside the door. Such hotel cases preceded the Matrimonial Causes Act of 1937, which made cruelty and desertion after five years independent grounds for divorce. Desertions soon accounted for half of all divorces. It is interesting that until 1923 60 per cent of divorce proceedings were taken by husbands, and thereafter the proportion reversed, with wives obtaining 60 per cent of divorces.

Increasingly, divorce came to be viewed as a legal mopping-up operation after the spiritual death of a marriage. A report by a Committee set up by the Archbishop of Canterbury (1966) recommended that the doctrine of the breakdown of marriage was preferable to that of the matrimonial offence. In 1969, a further step was taken away from contentious divorce. The Divorce Reform Act of that year introduced irretrievable breakdown of the marriage as the only ground for divorce. This is the current state of the law. But the breakdown still has to be evidenced by proving an 'offence' (adultery, desertion or unreasonable behaviour) unless the parties agree to divorce after living apart for two years, or live separately for five years if one party objects. There is increasing recognition of the emotional and financial costs of divorce, its effects on children, and how judicial processes may contribute to these.

In December 1993, this recognition found expression in a consultation paper for divorce reform (Law Commission 1993). The aims of the proposals for reform include supporting marriage by ensuring there is a period for the parties to reflect on the seriousness of the step they are planning to take, while minimizing acrimony for those who see no alternative to ending the marriage. The proposal is that the only ground for divorce should be a statement of irretrievable breakdown followed by a process of time: one year is the recommended period. A central plank of the proposed new procedures is a greater role for mediation than litigation in the divorce process. If the recommendations are accepted, fault will play no part in obtaining divorce. The Solicitors Family Law Association, which has worked since its inception in 1983 to counter adversarial confrontation in divorce, supports this move away from fault towards promoting conciliatory rather than litigious approaches, and concentrating on plans for the future rather than recriminations about the past.

The proposals are being criticized for making divorce easier. However, three-quarters of divorces are now sought on the facts of adultery or unreasonable behaviour, and less than one-fifth on separation after two years. Contested divorces are almost unheard of. Present procedures do not even require the attendance of the parties at court and can be completed in no more than three to four months. If the proposals take effect, four fifths of those getting divorced will have a longer period within which to reflect upon their decision.

And Marriage?

Lord Stowell declared in 1790 that 'the general happiness of the married life is secured by indissolubility'. In contrast, Milton believed that 'if mutual affection causes the matrimony, with good reason the contrary inclination, by mutual consent, should dissolve it.' These two opposing views on the dissolution of marriage continue to be expressed.

It is important to remember that divorce is not a disease but an attempted remedy for a disease. The disease lies within marriage. Divorce law cannot prevent marriage breakdown, nor can it be used as a prop to shore up the institution of marriage. What it can do is provide a dignified exit from a broken marriage. Calls for the reintroduction of fault and the matrimonial offence as the only true ground of divorce are not, I believe, an option. Couples need to be encouraged to look forward rather than to relive the past. The same applies to legislation; turning the legal clock back is not an answer to the problems of marriage.

While there are 170,000 divorces in the UK every year, there are also over 300,000 marriages. The majority of these will not end in divorce. Those that do may reflect heightened expectations of what each party should receive from the marriage contract. The ideals of marriage remain, and some are sustainable. To adapt a famous quotation: marriage might protest strongly on its behalf that the news of its demise has been somewhat exaggerated.

Jane Simpson

3
Marriage as Covenant

Marriage is one attempt at resolving the essential paradox of our individual, communal and social nature. The institution is deeply rooted in religious tradition in all cultures, and in modern Western society this means, in the main, the Judaeo-Christian tradition. Three concepts are of particular importance in the religious tradition: they are those of covenant, sacrament and contract.

In all the ancient religions there is felt to be a close connection between the marriages of humans and those made between the gods. In the Graeco-Roman world, for example, there is a lively family-life tradition among its gods and goddesses. For the Israelites, God is one, not many, and so it is the relationship between God and his people that is used as a paradigm for the central relationship between women and men in marriage.

This relationship is one of covenant. It is initiated and held in faithfulness by God, despite the often insufficient and inadequate response of His people. In this sense the covenant between God and Israel is asymmetrical. But it expects and needs a response from Israel, an acceptance of what has been initiated. Moreover, the covenant is something which is formally established in a public way – 'I will be your God, you shall be my people' – and it is made in order that a new relationship of love can be created, developed and fulfilled between the two parties. Atkinson (1979) summarizes the meaning of covenant as follows:

> By covenant is meant an agreement between two parties based on promise, which includes these four elements: first, an understanding of committed faithfulness made by one party to the other (or by each to the other); secondly, the acceptance of that undertaking by the other party; thirdly, public knowledge of such an undertaking and its acceptance; and fourthly, the growth of a personal relationship based on and expressive of such a commitment. (p.70)

This metaphor of covenant interacts both ways between marriage and the religious tradition. Marriage is understood as being in some sense reflective of the covenantal relationship between God and His people, but also, in turn, it provides metaphors for the relationship. Thus, Yahweh speaks to Israel through his prophet Jeremiah (2.2):

> I remember the devotion of your youth,
> your love as a bride
> how you followed me in the wilderness

In a different vein, the unhappiness of the prophet Hosea's marriage relationship is thought to have provided him with a sustained metaphor for castigating the faithlessness of Israel to their marriage covenant with God. Looking towards a more promising moment in time, Hosea (2.19–20) has God say:

> I will betroth you to myself for ever, betroth you in lawful wedlock with unfailing devotion and love. I will betroth you to myself to have and to hold and you shall know the Lord.

There are several important features of the concept of covenant. First, because it is initiated unilaterally, it is unconditional upon the other party's response, although in no way unaffected by it. Thus the faithlessness of Israel does not impair the covenant entered into between Israel and God, even though Israel's response is a cause of anger and sorrow. Second, it is a permanent commitment: once a covenant has been offered and accepted it cannot be *ended* even though it can be *broken*. Third, it does not require an outsider or third party to make it effective, although it is by its nature a publicly known promise and undertaking, and is marked by a sign – the rainbow after the Flood, for example, or circumcision to mark the enduring covenant with Abraham. A covenant is, however, created and sustained by the parties themselves.

There are parallel strands of thinking within the church: those of marriage as sacrament, marriage as contract and marriage as relationship. There is a sense in which, while the idea of marriage as covenant is a continuous theme throughout the Judaeo-Christian tradition, the idea of marriage as contract and marriage as sacrament represents the different emphases of the Protestant and Catholic religious traditions, respectively. The Anglican tradition talks of marriage as one of the 'commonly called sacraments', and the Reformed tradition tends to talk more about covenant than contract. In Roman Canon law, the older tradition of marriage as sacrament was overlaid upon the idea of marriage as covenant. Here we find that marriage is viewed as an outward and visible sign of an inward and invisible grace – a profound and permanent change of being that takes place between and within the couple. The two become in some ontological sense one, reflecting the 'one flesh' dictum of Genesis. The sacrament is effected by the couple themselves and is mediated by the mutual exchange of lifelong vows. Nevertheless, an essential ingredient in effecting the sacrament is normally the presence of a third party, the priest, who receives and confirms the vows made by the couple and signifies the couple's acceptance as a newly formed unit into the community of the church. There is, therefore, a parallel between the way in which the sacrament creates an inner change, and the way in which a marital contract is seen as conferring a new status.

The contractual side of a covenant is expressed most clearly by the ceremony through which it is initiated, and in marriage the contract between the parties is made explicit in the wedding. But a contract does not express all that is involved in a covenant, just as a wedding is not a marriage, for it is the promise of the fulfilling of the relationship in an ongoing contract between the two that is at the heart of the covenant.

Thus, marriage as relationship, so important an ingredient in our modern understanding of the institution, is also reflected in the earliest Judaeo-Christian religious traditions, and remains a continuing feature of a religious concept of marriage. Marriage may be perceived as an important part of the social, communal and religious fabric of life, but it is nothing if it is not also a personal relationship. Thus the poetry of the Song of Songs eloquently describes the relationship between lovers. We are also given glimpses of the way in which marriage could be a real love relationship in Israelite society. For example, when Hannah cries out in grief because of her childlessness, she is comforted by her husband Elkanah, which, considering the important emphasis on childbearing and family continuity in that society, has a remarkably modern relational ring: 'Am I not more to you than ten sons?' asks Elkanah (Samuel 1–9).

Throughout the history of the religious tradition this personal relationship is sometimes more evident than at others. Sometimes the functions of marriage are more clearly emphasized – as in the marriage service in the Anglican *Book of Common Prayer* of 1662. Sometimes the relational aspect is more clearly highlighted, as in the Anglican *Alternative Service Book* of 1980. But the relationship is always present as a continuing element.

Despite the fact that many people have lost direct contact with these early religious traditions, and marriage today is a strongly secular institution, it remains, I suspect, deeply imbued for most people with symbolic meaning derived from its earlier religious roots. Moreover, those who continue to be actively involved in a faith community remain deeply engaged with marriage as a religious institution which then holds for the participants an array of different meanings.

The church and the Jewish faith community continue to be deeply concerned with marriage, as well as influenced by the way in which it is currently understood by those outside the church. The church, society and the professional community of marriage specialists interact and influence one another in relation to the institution of marriage. Thus there continues to exist a spectrum of belief about the nature of marriage ranging from the indissolubilists at one end, to those who view marriage solely as a contract, albeit a contract which confers status, which can be ended unilaterally or by mutual consent. The third strand, which overlaps with the others and is interwoven within both the religious tradition and the legal framework, is that of marriage as relationship, and the knowledge and consequent understanding that relationships can and do die.

The notion of marriage as covenant has, I believe, a richness and complexity about it which can helpfully inform our thinking. Marriage viewed as covenant is, as noted earlier, a view that emphasizes the *unconditional, asymmetrical* and *permanent* nature of the new relationship. It is *unconditional* in the sense that it does not imply a bargain: it is not predicated upon the behaviour or assets of the other party. Thus the Christian marriage vow is one that is taken and made to the other 'for better, for worse, for richer for poorer, in sickness and in health'. The covenant is entered into unconditionally – in a sense profligately, because who would be so foolish as to bind themselves to so unconditional a contract? Yet it is this unconditional element that holds within it the very nature of marriage, something that is essential – that is of the very essence – of what love is about. One can argue from this conception of covenant that love in marriage has to be unconditional, otherwise it simply is not love.

Marriage as covenant is also *asymmetrical.* This does not mean that the marital relationship is asymmetrical between husband and wife. We may be only too familiar with the way in which the churches have tacitly condoned domestic violence and have apparently institutionalized its possibility by emphasizing, from St Paul onwards, the submission and obedience of the wife to her husband while neglecting St Paul's other word about mutual submission out of reverence for Christ. The meaning of covenant is quite other. The covenant relationship emphasizes the dual asymmetrical commitment to the marriage of each of the parties to it. *Each* party is the initiator of the covenant and *each* party takes the responsibility for sustaining the covenant, both with the other party and with the marital relationship itself.

Third, a covenant is *permanent* – it is 'until death do us part'. In an obvious way this concept may feel as if it leads only to an indissolubilist conclusion. If a covenant is permanent and marriage is a covenant, how can marriage ever be dissolved?

We are helped out of this impasse by a consideration of what Anderson and Guernsey (1985) call 'the irrevocable investment of affect'. By the nature of the relationship, an emotional investment accrues to those who have entered into a marital covenant. It is not that an external prohibition prevents the dissolution; it is that there are aspects of the covenanted relationship that remain indissoluble, even after a marital breakdown, because of the intrinsic nature of marriage (and, I suspect, of other committed relationships as well). The investments of affect and moral commitment to the other person do of course change radically after a marriage ends, and helping those changes take place in ways that lead to a constructive end is part of the business of a civilized society. However, it is also true that something enduring remains. This notion can help us to be more realistic and compassionate in the way we think about couples who continue in their marriages and couples who go through the trauma of bringing marriage to an end.

Sue Walrond-Skinner

4
My Partner, My Self?

When two people establish themselves as a couple, they do so for many different reasons and for a variety of purposes. Some of these are known about, thought about and talked about. Others are not; they are unconscious, but may be referred to by such familiar expressions as 'love at first sight', or the 'chemistry' of a relationship. These unconscious meanings and motivations are enacted and realized in the choice of partner and in the nature of the subsequent relationship mutually constructed by the two people concerned.

The Chemistry of Love Relations

As with the conscious reasons for coming together – similar interests, mutual aspirations and common understandings – unconscious meanings and motivations will be sufficiently shared to create a marital fit – colloquially expressed in expressions such as, 'my other half', or, perhaps more interesting, 'my better half'.

These sufficiently shared conscious and unconscious reasons and motivations will be in terms of supplementarity and complementarity. Some aspects of the other will be familiar and comparable to known parts of the self. They will supplement the sense of identity and therefore be comforting. Complementary aspects will apparently be quite unfamiliar and foreign. The very *difference* in the other becomes a source of attraction, generating excitement and interest based both on a sense of fascination and of fearfulness. All relationships will contain a mixture of both supplementary and complementary features.

Different couples will be able to manage different degrees of sameness and difference. For some, the safety of apparent similarity will be paramount; for others, the appeal and excitement of apparent differences will carry the higher premium. I purposefully use the adjective 'apparent' because choice of partner is based on both conscious and unconscious factors and meanings. The *apparently* unfamiliar may have a meaning and purpose which is common to both partners and is in effect shared between the two people. The *apparently* familiar may have a taken-for-granted quality, which creates an area of the couple's relationship that is never addressed, and can therefore become a repository for all kinds of anxiety-provoking differences which actually keep the couple separate and not known to each other.

Unconscious factors in a couple coming together and staying together will by definition never be known to them and need never be known. However, they can help us make sense of the attachment and affection, and of the tensions and conflicts in intimate relationships. It is to these unconscious factors that I refer when I speak of 'my partner my self': each partner unconsciously carrying for the other attributes and qualities that are similar to disowned or repressed parts of the self, and which are unconsciously related to in the other through identificatory mechanisms. In this way 'my partner, my self' refers to the psychological whole of each of the two individuals, with the relationship between them constituted substantially, although not wholly, by the attributes each identifies with and carries for the other. These attributes may therefore be said to be shared.

The emotional experience of there being something shared, something communal – not an unfamiliar sense to most couples in intimate relationships – is based on unconscious mechanisms that psychoanalysis describes as projection and identification. It constitutes the mutual attraction which brings a couple together initially and which then, unconsciously and consciously, influences and even dictates the nature of their subsequent interaction.

The Intrapsychic and the Interpersonal

Over the centuries philosophers, poets, political theorists, anthropologists, sociologists, psychologists, historians, novelists and others have all from their particular perspectives commented on the love relationship. Some have done so to celebrate it, some to criticize it, and many to attempt to study and understand its nature, meanings and purposes. This range of interest and scrutiny should not surprise us. The love relationship is both mysterious and ubiquitous. Its mystery attracts the poets, the novelists and the philosophers; its ubiquity attracts the anthropologists, the sociologists and the historians. What might a psychoanalytic perspective teach us about it?

The couple's love relationship pivots between the private selves of the individuals and their public self as represented by the other and by their need to relate to the other. It stands between internal reality and external reality, between what is inside and what is outside, between the intrapsychic and the interpersonal. The committed couple relationship is the arena *par excellence* for the expression of the constant and inevitable tensions between the individuality and autonomy necessary for the emotional health of each of the partners, and the equally necessary requirements of the relationship they are part of and aspire to. This constant interplay between separateness and togetherness is inherent in all human relationships, but may be felt most keenly in the intensity of love relationships.

The *interpersonal* dynamic of the twosome, influenced by the *intrapsychic* (internal) dynamics of each of the individuals, is yet further affected if into this two-person relationship there enters a third – a child – as a product and responsibility of the couple. The couple is then no longer simply a *sexual* couple but also a *parental* couple. The twosome then becomes a threesome, within which the needs of pairs continue to exist, be they the needs of the sexual couple, the nursing couple or the parent/child couple. Graphically, this twosome within the threesome dynamic may be depicted by a triangle, the three points of man, woman and child being joined by lines of emotional connection. The twosome-threesome dynamic contained within the triangle offers the opportunity, indeed the requirement, for experiences of inclusion and of exclusion (Britton, 1989). The capacity to tolerate being both part of something and not part of something constitutes psychological health. It is most obviously realized in the intensity of an intimate relationship.

Each Our Own Expert

Alongside the interests and perspective of the poets, the anthropologists and all the other commentators, there is one other who is probably more experienced and learned, and certainly more powerful in terms of influencing the nature of the couple relationship. That person is each one of us ourselves. Many of us are, or have been, or aspire to be, in a committed couple relationship. Some of us choose not to be. Certainly an increasing number choose not to have the relationship sanctioned by either church or state. But it is not at all clear that the couple relationship itself is less popular than it used to be.

Everyone by definition is the product of a couple, or perhaps more accurately, of coupling. We all have an experience or an idea of a couple, even if it is only in our minds. This psycho-biological fact is beyond dispute. It is a fact which constructs a constitutional preconception of linking and relating that is realized immediately upon birth by the infant's hungry mouth searching for the mother's nipple, by the necessary relating to maternal and paternal figures, and, of course, by the earliest and most primitive awareness of the parental couple relationship, even if this only involves the absent father being in the mind of the present caretaking mother.

From the very beginning, therefore, the blueprint of expectations and assumptions which builds up within us always results from and is in relation to interactive processes. The constitutional preconception of linking and relating meets the fact of experienced interaction inherent in our development from birth. In psychoanalytic writings, the psychoanalyst and paediatrician Donald Winnicott is often quoted as saying that ' "there is no such thing as a baby" – meaning that if you set out to describe a baby, you will find you are describing a *baby and someone*. A baby cannot exist alone, but is essentially part of a relationship.' (Winnicott, 1964, p.88) This, of course, refers to the very particular and special case of an infant and his or her mother. However, the same is true for all human beings throughout their lives.

Everyone, therefore, from their own inevitable, although varied, experience is very familiar with couples and couple relationships. In this way, everyone is an expert, both through their internal images (hopes and fears) of the nature of relationships and the realities of their external social interaction. Because of this, it sometimes feels difficult or even provocative to address the subject of marriage.

Idealization and Denigration

Most of us know from our experiences and from our observations of others that the couple relationship is not and cannot be perfect. We are aware of a tendency either to idealize marriage or – and more so in the last two or three decades – to denigrate it in blanket terms. It seems difficult to maintain a degree of balance.

Robert Louis Stevenson wrote that, 'Marriage is like life in this – that it is a field of battle and not a bed of roses.' This image of the 'battle of life' is not in my view a criticism, but a description of the inevitable, necessary and potentially creative and healthy conflict inherent in any human interaction. All intimate relationships, if they are to survive and develop, have to manage the tension between feelings of love and satisfaction and those of anger and disappointment. The psychoanalytic perspective may be helpful in thinking about this because from its very beginnings it has been theoretically based on the notion of dynamic conflict, both within and between individuals. For this reason, among others, it may be a particularly useful framework within which to consider the 'battlefield' of marriage.

It should be noted that one aspect of the definition of that particularly hard to define concept of maturity, and mature relating, is tolerance of ambivalence: the capacity to hold contradictory feelings – feelings of love and feelings of hate – in relation to the same person. The word 'ambivalence' is often used pejoratively, and yet it is also considered to be one of the attributes of mental health.

Even against this background of acknowledging, and indeed stressing, the inevitable conflicts in intimate relationships, it may at times appear as if I am describing the couple relationship as if it were, or had the potential to be, an ideal state. Although I do hold a view of the developmental potential inherent in a good-enough couple relationship, I do not think of it as an ideal state; no such state exists in the real world.

The tendency to idealize or denigrate the marital state is worth reflecting on. Why is it that marriage can sometimes provoke such strong interest and reactions from so many different quarters – let alone from the participants in the relationship itself? From this question we begin to move towards the heart of the matter.

Perhaps the idealization and denigration of marriage emerges inevitably from the potential nature of the relationship itself: as an intimate, committed, long-term attachment that is central to people's lives. Freud is quoted as saying that an averagely healthy individual has the capacity 'to love and to work'. Erikson (1956) writes;

> It pays to ponder on this simple formula; it gets deeper as you think about it. For when Freud said 'love' he meant *genital* love, and genital *love*; when he said love *and* work, he meant a general work-productiveness which would not preoccupy the individual to the extent that he loses his right or capacity to be a genital and a loving being. (p.256)

The suggestion being made is that the opportunity and capacity for love and genital love are of profound importance for establishing and maintaining psychological health.

The committed adult sexual relationship, an emotional and physical relationship, may well contain the potential for feelings and experiences of the deepest intimacy and intensity, second only to the relationship between an infant and parent, usually mother. The mother-infant relationship is the first relationship which includes the desire and need for intimacy, commitment, dependence and sufficient attention being paid to both emotional and physical states.

Through good-enough attention being paid to the infant's physical and emotional needs, growth and development are nurtured, and the infant begins the long process of realizing whatever potential he or she may have. Metaphorically, this is a way in which the potential of marriage can also be described. Potentially, the marital relationship offers the possibility of regressing to a childlike or infantile state as in the expression of dependence, need and attachment, or in playful sexuality. Equally, it obliges the more mature self to emerge in responding to the needs of the partner and, perhaps most particularly, to the needs of any children they may have.

In this context the potential for idealizing and denigrating marriage is based on the often unconscious, although sometimes known about, ambivalence towards intimate relationships rooted in our very first experiences of intimacy, usually with our mothers and fathers. Mothers, fathers and parents as a couple can at best only ever be good-enough. Inevitably, therefore, everyone, from their infant beginnings, has to cope with frustration and disappointment, as well as enjoying comfort, satisfaction and pleasure. The provision of average good-enough care from our parental environment, which includes experiences of frustration (and therefore hate) as well as satisfaction (and therefore love), meets with our own internal potential for feeling good and bad. In this way, our inherent capacity to experience conflict is moulded and further built upon through our actual experiences from the very beginning.

By stating this, particularly by referring to our inherent capacity for experiencing feelings of goodness and badness from the very beginning, I am inviting a debate on the nature of human destructiveness and evil, and how these relate to the nature of marriage.

Temperley (1984) writes about the phenomenon very well. There is, she says, what may be called a somewhat utopian view which attributes evil to the nature of social and cultural organization, and believes that if that were altered, human nature, which this view holds is naturally benign, would then be freed to express itself in a benevolent way. The other view, to which some schools of psychoanalysis adhere (as does the Christian doctrine of Original Sin), stresses the unchanging nature of the struggle between good and evil within each one of us. With this view, if we are to improve our social relations, and especially marriage, we must take full and proper cognizance of the internal origins of love and hate. Mature love may be described as including an acknowledgement of the flawed nature of both the self and the loved other, and as including a capacity for tolerance and forgiveness. Less mature love will be marked by violent swings between love and hate, with the self and the other being seen either as only loving or only hateful. We may all aspire towards more mature love, but inevitably we will all at times find ourselves overcome by idealistic love or denigratory hatred.

The central issue then becomes finding the means of managing this inevitable conflict both within ourselves and between ourselves and others. And, of course, the more intimate the other is, the more intense will be the feelings of both love and hate. The pain of betrayal, a major source of hatred and outrage, comes from having loved and trusted. We are not betrayed by our enemies, but by those whom we love and whom we had assumed loved us (Mattinson, 1993). Henry Dicks, a psychoanalyst who wrote one of the earliest definitive works on marriage and psychoanalytic marital psychotherapy, asserted that, 'the opposite to love is not hate. These two always co-exist so long as there is a live relationship. The opposite to love is indifference.' (1967, p.133)

Freud (1921), perhaps inevitably, had already alerted us to this when in his psychoanalytic writings he referred to what he called the death instinct, a potential towards destructiveness which resides in each one of us, alongside a life instinct which promotes creativity:

> . . . almost every intimate emotional relation between two people which lasts for some time – marriage, friendship, the relations between parents and children – contains a sediment of feelings of aversion and hostility, which only escapes perception as a result of represssion. (p.101)

Marriage as a Transference Relationship

From the very beginning, then, we have to build up various emotional means whereby we are able to deal with the inevitable frustration and pain of living. Defences become those means through which we construct and experience ourselves and our relationships. The experiencing of thoughts and feelings in current relationships and situations which derive from aspects of the thoughts and feelings first occurring in relation to previous significant figures and experiences is called transference.

Gosling (1968) writes:

> Falling in love is perhaps one of the most striking examples of transference . . . In a marriage relationship each partner is constantly to some extent reacting to the other as if the other were a figure out of his past life, or he is trying to get the other to behave

like a figure out of his imagination, be it a consciously known figure or a kind of ghost or shadow-figure who is constantly but unconsciously expected . . . (pp.4–5)

The ways in which transferences are dealt with in a couple relationship are varied and complex. (Spouses, of course, do not think of transferences, but are likely to be aware of familiar patterns which arise between them, some of which may even be recognized as originating from earlier experiences in their lives.) In a developmental marriage they are sometimes accepted and sometimes rejected. When rejected, the transferrer is faced with a different reality. If this new reality is accepted, it may soften and mediate internal images and external expectations; the relationship can then move on. The recipient of a transference will also have internal images and expectations, and will therefore respond with both conscious and unconscious parts of the self. The rhythm, style and content of this mutual transferential dynamic makes up the marital dance, which is sometimes in harmony, sometimes stumbling, sometimes rather clumsy, and sometimes cruelly stepping on the other's toes.

The couple relationship can therefore be thought of as a mutual transference relationship. Each partner may, usually unconsciously, identify with and promote aspects of their partner which are either similar to or very different from how the self is viewed. The strongest bond between a couple is likely to be the harmony of their unconscious internal images of patterns of relating (Ruszczynski, 1993). Each partner will represent or characterize for the other a repressed or split-off part of the self. Even quite dissimilar partners may find in each other what they have most sternly repressed in themselves. The psychological processes which bring this about are called projective and introjective identification (Klein, 1946). These are unconscious mental mechanisms whereby aspects of the self and internal images are in part provoked and related to in the other as if they were part of the other. This is, of course, a mutual process present in all relationships. By mutually receiving one another's unconscious expectations, each partner gives the other an initial feeling of acceptance and attachment, and then provides their part of the marital choreography.

This externalization of internal ambivalence and conflict into someone who has to be contended with each day may enable that part of the personality which had been felt to be unmanageable or intolerable (and therefore split-off and projected outside the self) to become more comfortably related to within the self. However, it may also produce a fierce fight to control or punish that aspect in the partner. Tensions within a couple relationship can in this way be understood as the externalization and enactment of shared internal conflicts (Ruszczynski, 1992). Of course, loving and creative expectations and experiences are also re-enacted in the couple relationship. Partners then recreate in their relationship, for themselves and each other, internalized benevolent experiences and expectations.

This, then, may be said to be what constitutes the developmental potential in marriage and other committed couple relationships – a new opportunity is created to resolve and work through earlier fears and conflicts associated with intimacy. This is at the heart of the unconscious or secret contract in marriage.

The Secret Contract

Mr and Mrs Smith sought help for their marriage following a number of minor suicide attempts by Mrs Smith. It was learned that Mr Smith had a long history of bereavements throughout his life, culminating in the recent death of his mother. The depression, mourning and sense of loss which one might have expected in these circumstances was, however, noticeably absent. Mrs Smith, in contrast, was depressed, although it was not possible at first to understand why. As a couple they presented a rather rigid picture of a strong husband and vulnerable wife, although there was also a sense of fragility, which was at first understood by their therapists to relate to fears and anxieties produced by the suicide attempts.

It quickly became apparent how Mr Smith avoided and deflected any issues which might provoke in him feelings of discomfort, pain or loss. It also became clear how Mrs Smith was party to these avoidances: she would often introduce her own fears and anxieties just as her husband began to approach difficult and painful areas of his experience, diverting attention away from her husband to herself.

This particularly tense marital dance was enacted totally unconsciously by the couple, and initially included the therapists as well. They found themselves behaving with the couple as the couple related to each other: unconsciously, they, too, accepted the invitation to focus on Mrs Smith rather than stay with the painful feelings being brought nearer to consciousness for Mr Smith.

It appeared that the couple could not focus on Mr Smith's anxieties, but had an unconscious agreement to attend to what worried Mrs Smith. It eventually emerged that the couple shared the view that if Mr Smith was to let himself know about the losses he had experienced he would not be able to bear the feelings that would be stirred up in him, and that he might go mad or kill himself. For this reason the depression that Mr Smith feared was being projected into his wife, and she was unconsciously willing to carry it because she feared the consequences of not doing so. It also emerged that the couple shared a phantasy that women's strength was gained at the expense of men. Mrs Smith had an unconscious fear that if she openly demonstrated her strengths her husband would in some way suffer or be damaged as a consequence. The couple therefore constructed a relationship which had the appearance of the strong husband and vulnerable wife, and which served them both in allowing them to avoid that which they separately feared. Simultaneously, however, it also perpetuated the very fears they sought to allay.

As long as Mr Smith rid himself of his sense of vulnerability by projecting it into his wife, and she, for her own reasons, was prepared unconsciously to accept it, the resulting relationship appeared to be that of the strong husband and vulnerable wife. This allowed him to deal with his unconscious fears about his vulnerabilities, and her to deal with her fears about her strengths. Equally, as long as Mrs Smith continued to invite these projections from her husband, and he responded to her invitation, unconsciously each experienced this as a confirmation of his vulnerability and need to be rescued, and of her strength and capacity to manage painful feelings. Further, this strength of Mrs Smith's continued to be experienced by both partners as destructively undermining of Mr Smith by colluding with the phantasy that he could not manage his anxieties for himself. This particular marital dance dealt with the couple's anxieties defensively, but it also perpetuated them and deprived them both of the opportunity to test whether vulnerability and strength need necessarily be destructive or dangerous.

In their families of origin, Mr and Mrs Smith had both had vulnerable fathers: hers owing to long-term unemployment, and his to a serious and disabling physical illness. Neither of the fathers could bear to know about their vulnerabilities and were protected from doing so by wives who exercized their care in subtle ways that appeared not to undermine the external image of the men. Mr and Mrs Smith each recalled memories of having to behave in ways that avoided saying or doing things which might expose their father's vulnerability. Such messages left them both with a phantasy that they could hurt or damage their fathers.

For both the Smith's, therefore, the internalized experience was that men had to be protected and women were to protect them without their knowing. The shared phantasy (Bannister and Pincus, 1965) enacted by this couple was, in simple terms, that the vulnerability of men and the strength of women could not consciously be known about and acknowledged because to do so would risk damaging the men, whose sense of self would be substantially threatened. It was just as necessary for Mr Smith to deny his vulnerability as it was for Mrs Smith to deny her capacity to manage. Acknowledging either would for this couple signal danger to the man. The couple's initial unconscious attraction to each other, and the rhythm of their subsequent relating was in part based on the commonality of this internal image of the nature of relationships between men and women.

In this chapter I have suggested that alongside the conscious hopes and aspirations which bring a couple together there are powerful unconscious attractions and motivations, substantially informed by sufficiently shared internal images, conflicts and expectations. This unconscious attraction is brought about by mutual identificatory processes whereby aspects of the other, which have an unconscious meaning for the self, are unconsciously experienced (identified with) as if they were aspects of the self residing in the other. My partner is then experienced as my self, or my other selves, and aspects of my self are located only in my partner.

These dynamics produce what I have referred to as a marital dance, with the couple jointly but unconsciously negotiating the emotional footwork involved. The intimacy, longevity and commitment of marriage makes it a particularly powerful relationship within which to attend both to unresolved aspects of one's inner world as well as to repeat and build on satisfying experiences from the past in a contemporary relationship.

Stanley Ruszczynski

5
The Companionship Trap

All is not well in the state of marriage – or, at least, that seems to be a widespread view. There is much discussion of our 'high' divorce rate, the rise of cohabitation and the number of children born outside marriage, which now approaches one-third of all births. It is suggested that marriage is not providing the satisfaction and support it once did. Society seems to have lost its way – that, at least, is the claim. The causes of these changes are usually perceived as a shift in marital behaviour and attitudes and not, for example, a result of changing economic and social pressures on couples. So it is more likely that the so-called 'sexual revolution' of the 1960s will be cited as a cause rather than the present economic recession, with its accompanying housing crisis and high rates of unemployment.

In this chapter I want to stand aside from these current debates and draw on the work of social scientists and historians to see how far these perspectives may illuminate the current debate. But before doing this, it is worth commenting on what is seen as 'the problem'.

As with so many public debates about domestic life, the current one presents marriage and divorce in over-general terms and exaggerates the difficulties. It is widely believed that the divorce rate in the UK is rapidly rising; in fact, it has been broadly stable since the mid-1970s (Elliott, 1991). The rate itself is modest compared with many countries (Goode, 1993) – for example, the US or any of the Scandinavian countries, where the matter is complicated by very high rates of cohabitation which are now making marriage a minority status for adults who live as a couple. It also remains the fact that, on current projections, about two-thirds of existing marriages will end with the death of one or other spouse. Divorce rates are, in fact, widely variable within the UK: while those of south-east England may be relatively high in the European Community league, Northern Ireland has one of the lowest rates in Europe. I am not suggesting there have been no changes in the UK. For instance, cohabitation is now a common phenomenon and is accepted by many in ways in which it certainly was not a generation ago (see Chapter 1). But while there are significant and important changes, they are, in part at least, the result of long-term processes that have been operating for a century or more, rather than indicating sudden recent change (Richards and Elliott, 1991; Reibstein and Richards, 1992).

My second point is that not all change is in the same direction. Over the last few decades we have seen a striking rise in what may broadly be called fundamentalism in at least three of the major religions in Britain: Christianity, Islam and Judaism. These movements have focused on issues related to marriage and family life and are now a potent force, pushing for what they regard as traditional values. Prominent among these are opposition to divorce and cohabitation.

The Companionship Trap

Since the earliest days of marriage research, there has been an interest in divorce. The logic behind the research is straightforward enough: it attempted to isolate factors characterizing marriages that ended in divorce with the aim that these could be used as a basis for intervention – either to head-off particularly vulnerable marriages, or to provide better help and support for those in trouble. Looking back over what is now more than half a century of such research in North America and Europe, one would have to say that the results have been rather disappointing.

What this kind of research has succeeded in doing has been to confirm a number of common-sense notions about marriage, but it has provided little by way of understanding. So we know that if spouses are particularly young or old, or the wife is pregnant at her wedding or conceives very soon afterwards, the marriage is more likely than others to end in divorce, as are marriages where there is a wide gap between spouses, whether this is in age, social background, culture or religion. Spouses who marry after a relatively brief acquaintance, or who do so against the wishes of their families, are more likely to divorce. Once married, factors such as economic hardship, prolonged absence of a spouse from the house because of work, large numbers of children, or none at all, and overt conflict all show the links with divorce that one might expect (Raschke, 1987).

Of course, it may be that this research has simply chosen to look at the more obvious factors, and so not surprisingly has confirmed what we believed all along. Or perhaps there is little to be learnt at this level of analysis. Maybe once we have dealt with the obvious potential sources of conflict and friction, there is not much more that can be said. It is certainly true that research is now moving away from the demographic level of analysis, and, as illustrated by the other contributors to this volume, there is more of interest to be said about such matters as the beliefs that spouses bring to their marriage, and their styles of relating to one another.

My intention here is to develop a rather different perspective, and I want to take the historical correlation between divorce rates and the rise of companionate marriage as the starting point for my argument (Phillips, 1988). What I suggest is that this is not a chance association: companionate marriage is in itself unstable, and it contains the roots of its own destruction. Rather than offering a 'haven in a heartless world', its apparent safety is an illusion which for some will become the bitterness and recriminations of divorce. To simplify an argument that necessarily deals with very complex matters, I will confine my discussion to middle-class marriage in Britain.

Some History

What has become known as 'companionate marriage' has its origins in the middle-class domestic world that developed during the Industrial Revolution (Reibstein and Richards, 1992). It is a system of marriage based on individual choice of partner and romantic love and became well established by the end of the last century. It is a notion of marriage in which the two partners, ideally at least equal in position, set out to share all their domestic life together: each becomes not only a lover, but companion, friend and confidant, with whom most or all leisure time is spent. However, while this ideal of companionate marriage laid emphasis on the equal and complementary roles of men and women, it developed in a world in which domestic life was widely segregated. Men centred their life in the world of work and politics; women were expected to confine their interests to their homes and a domestic social world. The contradiction that this produced remains central in marriage today.

As one might expect in a period of change, issues related to marriage were widely debated in the closing decade of the last century and the first two of the present, leaving a rich source for those interested in the development of modern marriage.

A common line of argument was that the institution of marriage was in itself stifling and antithetical to love. This theme is one that is prominent in the novels of the period (see Chapter 6) – as one fictional character puts it when speaking of love and marriage, why would people want to cook porridge in a Greek vase? A common suggestion was that state and societal control of marriage made it unnecessarily restrictive in ways that damaged the relationship of the spouses. For example, in *Halcyon, or The Future of Monogamy* (Britten, 1929), the author argued that more freedom in the form of such things as better sex education, freer access to contraception, and easier divorce for those who made mistakes in their choice of partner would improve marriage, together with better economic and educational opportunities for women.

Perhaps typical of a slightly earlier period was *Modern Marriage and How To Bear It* (Churton Braby, 1909). This argues for a marriage based on affection and respect, avoiding passion on the one hand and mere convenience on the other. She suggests that before marriage, women need to know something of the world, men and sex. She extols the virtues of the 'preliminary canter' or 'ante-hymeneal fling', but is quick to point out that women should not sow their wild oats quite as literally as men. However, she is not unsympathetic to those who do:

. . . a woman – new style – who has knocked about one half of the world and sown a mild crop of the delectable cereal will prove a far better wife, a more cheery friend and faithful comrade. (p.29)

. . . a good woman who has surrendered herself to an ardent lover and has been deserted by him must necessarily have gone through such intense suffering that her character is probably deepened thereby and her capacity for love and faithfulness increased. (p.32)

Within marriage, this author's expectation is of a continuing double standard. She states that if men are faithful, it is only because of lack of opportunity and disinclination. But however close a friendship and companionship she recommends, she does not believe there should be no secrets in marriage, and she comments that few men are sufficiently 'lacking in wisdom to let a wife discover their misconduct'. She also addresses the issue of monogamy for women, but in a less direct way, through the imagined institution of 'duogamy', in which women would have two husbands. Her fictional characters discuss the advantages of this and point out how their interests are much wider than those of men. An obvious interpretation of this would be to see it as a reflection of the way that women were still largely excluded from the male worlds of work and politics, and that domestic life represented a larger part of their social world than it did for men.

Important changes took place in middle-class domestic life in the 1920s and 1930s. Servants were now much less common, and, if present, were more likely to be a 'daily help' than one who lived in. Women undertook more of the domestic work and child care. Inevitably, this brought their husbands into closer contact with this work, but there is little indication that they shared in it beyond occasionally helping out at times of crisis. Although a division of labour remained, the social sphere was now a shared one, and this was true both within the home and outside it. I would suggest that an important and growing feature of marriage in this period was the way in which couples spent more time together. Shared leisure activities – involving public entertainment such as the cinema, or based on freely available public transport – increased in popularity, and much of this activity would also include the children. This was an era, recorded by many a box Brownie, that established the nuclear family as a social unit.

The Second World War, like the First, led to new attitudes and behaviour in relation to marriage. Women achieved more social and economic freedom, which seemed further to reinforce the idea of marriage as a shared and equal enterprise. The post-war era of prosperity allowed much fuller expression of such ideals. It is often assumed that the 1960s mark some kind of sudden break in marital and sexual relationships. I believe this view to be mistaken. While it may be true that at this time it became possible to speak more freely in public, and probably in private too, about sexual and relationship matters, changes in conduct were simply the continued development of trends that have a much longer history.

The point may be illustrated by changes in the sexual manuals. The old standards, like *Ideal Marriage: Its Physiology and Technique* (Van de Valde, 1928), which was first published in 1920, began to disappear. These were books that were explicitly addressed to married couples (although the unmarried were doubtless an important readership), and dealt with sex from an anatomical and mechanical point of view. They assumed men to be initiators, but counselled them to be mindful of the needs of their partners. Their replacement titles – for example *The Joy of Sex* (Comfort, 1974), are books of a very different kind, which present diverse sexual activities as pleasure for the mind and body, and make no assumptions about the marital status of participants.

Trends that had been growing throughout the century meant that by the 1960s the great majority of couples had experienced sexual intercourse before marriage (Reibstein and Richards, 1992). For most of these, it was no longer restricted to premarital sex for a couple who intended to marry, but the experience of a number of sexual relationships in which marriage may not have been part of the agenda for either participant.

Present Dilemmas

This history, outlined in skeletal form, has left us with a form of marriage that is, I believe, flawed, and with deep contradictions that lead to an instability that may be indexed by divorce. It is also reflected in the move by some to replace marriage by cohabitation. Ironically, the usual forms of cohabitation are based on very similar assumptions to marriage, and so lead to the same problems. It is not the marriage vows that cause the problems, but our assumptions about marriage and other couple relationships. Love, as writers of popular songs have long recognized, can neither cook meals nor wash clothes – but can it be the central ideology for a satisfactory marriage? Essentially that is the position it has come to occupy in historical middle-class marriage. But I would argue that the difficulties already perceived at the turn of the century in combining love and marriage have only become deeper.

Autonomy and the Shared Life

Central to the idea of companionate marriage is a shared life. But, as many commentators have described, there is a conflict between the need to construct a relationship based on the notion of a shared life and the desire for individual autonomy, which our modern culture also values highly. Askham (1984), for example, has provided a detailed analysis of the ways in which couples try to find a path between these competing values.

Another way of looking at the same set of issues is to see what happens when couples begin to have children. Although their number may be reduced, having children remains a central priority in modern marriage. Indeed, probably a larger proportion of all women (and, presumably, of men) have children today than in the recent past. Studies of marital satisfaction show that, typically, the high rates found in the first phase of marriage drop sharply as soon as children arrive. The effect is specifically related to the arrival of children and is not simply an effect of the increasing duration of marriage. Why should this be? Why should the achievement of what is still widely regarded as an objective of marriage have this effect? I would suggest three major reasons.

Most women give up paid work when they have children, at least for a time, and they begin to undertake a much greater proportion of the domestic work. The ideal of a shared life, in which both have jobs and domestic work is divided equally between them, can no longer be sustained. The advent of children makes plain the role segregation and the division of labour for men and women.

The second reason is, of course, that the care of children in our society is both time-consuming and often exhausting. This is well illustrated by the depression that so often is part of our modern institution of motherhood. Parenthood also brings changes in the couples' social world, especially for a mother who may lose the friendships associated with her employment. To some extent this may be compensated for by the development of other social networks, for instance with other women with children, and often a reinforcement of relationships with female kin, including their own mother. Despite this, many studies describe an isolated and rather lonely world for mothers of young children.

The third reason I would suggest is that children intrude into the shared and exclusive intimacy that forms part of the ideal of modern marriage. Leisure time – already reduced – has now to incorporate children and their needs. Finding space and time for a couple to be alone together will often involve making complicated arrangements. At a more subtle level, the experiences each bring to their common time may now be more divergent – one from a world of work, the other from nappies and babies. Polly Garter, in Dylan Thomas's (1954) *Under Milk Wood*, might have been speaking of the experience of married motherhood when she said, 'nothing grows in my garden, only washing. And babies.' This is very different from the romantic and exclusive honeymoon period of a marriage.

Sex Before and After Marriage

As already mentioned, most people now enter marriage having had experience of earlier sexual relationships. Sex is no longer held to be exclusive to marriage. This means that marriage has to be marked off in other ways from other relationships. This we may see in attitudes towards sexual exclusiveness, which have become more strongly expressed with the growth of the notion of companionate marriage. Even over the last few decades, we may discern a trend towards married people placing a stronger emphasis on monogamy (Reibstein and Richards, 1992).

We make more fuss over weddings than we used to; they have become more expensive in real terms and are more important socially. It seems we need to mark the change in status more clearly in public, and to underline that marriage is something different from the cohabitation(s) that may have preceded it.

But despite the attempts to mark off marriage from other relationships and the emphasis on monogamy, such evidence as we have suggests that over recent decades affairs have become more rather than less common (Reibstein and Richards, 1992). While the double standards of the Victorians may now take rather different forms, the evidence, such as it is – and it is sketchy to say the least – suggests that men are still more likely than women to have affairs.

Several different kinds of factors have probably contributed to the rising number of affairs: changing patterns of employment, especially for women, and leisure provide more opportunities for meeting potential extramarital partners; easy availability of effective contraception, backed up by abortion, has made the control of fertility more complete outside as well as within marriage. The married, like the unmarried, may share the same assumptions that close affectional relationships should be sexual and that the expression of sexuality is important to personal development. Having had a number of relationships based on such assumptions before marriage, it may prove difficult, despite intentions of monogamy, to avoid continuing the same patterns after the wedding.

So, at a time when monogamy for both men and women is particularly emphasized in marriage, there may be factors that draw the married into other sexual relationships. Ironically, the emphasis on sexuality as a central and integral part of any relationship makes an affair more threatening to a marriage than it may have been in the past. Such a shift can be documented in the changing patterns of advice offered in the 'problem pages' of women's magazines. While in the 1950s a wife with an erring husband was advised to be patient and to wait until he came to his senses, a present-day spouse is much more likely to be told that something is basically wrong with the marital relationship, and urgent action is required (Richards and Elliott, 1991). An added complication is that the nature of affairs may also have changed. Like marriage, the affair may also be companionate; and a companionate affair always poses the risk that it may become a companionate marriage.

Openness and Secrecy

Just as there was wide segregation in the roles of the Victorian middle-class marriage where couples would spend a considerable part of their leisure as well as work time apart, so there was often a degree of formality and distance in their relationship. There was no expectation that all confidences should be shared. Indeed, as can be seen from the marriage manuals of the period and the early decades of this century, the advice was not to share everything. Today the emphasis is very different. Shared confidences are very much a part of what is held to be a good and satisfactory marital relationship. Conversely, a failure to communicate and to share is seen in itself to be a marital problem that requires attention. To put it in rather different terms, the pendulum has swung towards a position where the expectation of companionate marriage is that autonomy is reduced and the idea of a merged intimacy is premium.

Much can be, and has been, said about exactly where the balance of intimacy and individual autonomy should lie. The point I want to emphasize is the difficulty that the expectation of openness and honesty can create when either spouse becomes involved in other relationships. The evidence suggests that most affairs remain secret. This poses an additional threat as they break the trust of openness on which modern marriage is based. As the authors of a book on American marriage comment, 'marriage makes couples more deceptive' (Blumstein and Schwartz, 1983). For those who work therapeutically with couples, there are obvious problems that arise in connection with the ways in which marital secrets are dealt with.

In this chapter I have tried to suggest that the evolution of modern marriage is such that it contains some fundamental contradictions. Necessarily, the argument has been very condensed, and it has not been possible to do full justice either to the historical material or to the complexities of modern marriage. In particular I have discussed marriage in broad terms and have not fully reflected its variety, the very different experience of men and women and of those in varying social and economic circumstances. However, the broad sweep does have the advantage of focusing attention on issues that will arise for all couples.

Of course, marriages are dynamic relationships that change over time. Each spouse brings a series of beliefs and expectations about marriage to their relationship, and together they begin to construct a shared reality in the light of those beliefs and those held by members of their social world (Berger and Kellner, 1964). The process of construction will be influenced in many ways by their social and economic position. In the course of the development of their relationship they must find resolutions for the contradictions that I have outlined. Many couples, of course, do this successfully – in the sense that they find a way of conducting their relationship that is more or less satisfactory for both of them. Others do not, and seek alternative partners or other patterns of relationship. We need to continue to analyse the formation and dissolution of marital relationships and the social context within which this occurs, so that we may become more realistic about one of the most central of our social institutions.

Martin Richards

6
Two Marriages in Fiction

Works of fiction often show insights into the lives of the characters created by their authors in ways that parallel insights derived by psychologists and psychotherapists in their work with those who consult them. In this chapter I shall use the two important marriages described in *Middlemarch* and *The Forsyte Saga* to illuminate aspects of the interior of marriage which are as relevant to our understanding of marital problems today as they may have been when the works were written.

Both marriages attest to the enduring nature of the intimacy of relationships between men and women, as well as to the unchanging predicaments and dilemmas that couples experience in their attempts to deal with emotional conflicts that marriage recreates and the opportunities for new solutions that it may offer. Each ends in failure, having been unsuccessful in resolving the problems set by the psychological conflicts which the couples brought to them. Nevertheless, failure may be seen as a step on the way to solving problems. Both novelists show this to be true for the two women in their later partnerships – although not for the men.

While it is possible to look at the dynamic issues within these marriages as expressions of the psychological problems experienced by the authors, it may be more illuminating to look at the lives of the characters in the novels as if they are living couples. By doing so, I believe it is possible to arrive at psychological truths of general relevance to living individuals and couples.

Dorothea and Casaubon[1]

The story begins before we are aware of Dorothea's interest in Casaubon. She is introduced at length in the first chapter of *Middlemarch*, and is compared in beauty and simplicity of dress with the Blessed Virgin as portrayed by Italian painters, which may already suggest some suppression of sensuality and sexuality. Although the unadorned attire of Dorothea and her younger sister, Celia, is ascribed to their breeding, religious feeling and a social awareness which 'regarded frippery as the ambition of the huckster's daughter' (p.29), so far as Dorothea is concerned, the reason lies deeper than that. Her denial of 'the solicitudes of feminine fashion', which appeared 'an occupation for Bedlam', is coupled with her being 'likely to seek martyrdom, to make retractions, and then to incur martyrdom after all in a quarter where she had not sought it.' (p.30)

Although George Eliot does not specifically make the link between a rather sombre style of dress and approach to life and Dorothea's early history, she nevertheless refers in the same paragraph to the loss of her parents when she was about 12 years old. The cause and circumstances of their deaths are not described, but it could be inferred that this was a sufficiently traumatic experience to ascribe Dorothea's ascetic lifestyle not only to a protest at the female role dictated by contemporary social mores, but also to depression. By including it in the same paragraph, the author is making the association unconsciously, as the contiguity of material in a chain of associations may be regarded as being unconsciously linked.

Dorothea is interested in improving the lot of the poor, and particularly of the tenants of her uncle's estate. It seems possible that this concern, which is not shared by other members of her family or land-owning neighbours, may be evidence of a reparative wish based upon a repressed feeling of guilt whose origin is not disclosed, but which accords with her sense of denial and depression. Since she was a little girl, Dorothea had nurtured a feeling that she would like 'to be of help to some one who did great works, so that his burthen might be lighter.' (p.399) This can be read as a reference to her father and to a displaced Oedipal wish, which became fixated as a result of the trauma of his death when she was on the threshold of puberty.

That Dorothea's puritanical denial of 'feminine frippery' goes deeper than social or religious sentiments might require is illustrated by an exchange with her sister about their mother's inherited jewellery: Dorothea is persuaded that it will be in order for Celia to wear these jewels, but resists any attempt to induce her to wear them herself. However, we are made aware of the possible breach in her defences against femininity when she sees her mother's diamond and emerald ring and matching bracelet:

'They are lovely,' said Dorothea, slipping the ring and bracelet on her finely-turned finger and wrist, and holding them towards the window on a level with her eyes. All the while her thought was trying to justify her delight in the colours by merging them in her mystic religious joy. (p.36)[2]

So we are made aware that not only is Dorothea repressing a

conventional display of her femininity, but also that the repression is incomplete, and a counter-wish is not far below the surface. Further evidence of this is found in her patent sexual attraction to men which she displaces on to her sister: '. . . if any gentleman appeared to come to The Grange from some other motive than that of seeing Mr Brooke, she concluded that he must be in love with Celia . . .' (p.32) The conflict between these two factors is then delicately sketched out, setting the scene for the two relationships Dorothea makes as the story unfolds. That the repression is uppermost at the beginning of her story is made evident in a refusal of an offer of marriage from Sir James Chettam, and her acceptance of the Reverend Mr Casaubon.

Casaubon is a clergyman, and a scholar of doubtful status. He is 50 years old, and a bachelor without any previous relationships with women, as he declares in a pedantic way in his characteristically unpassionate letter to Dorothea asking her to marry him. He appears to be physically unattractive and, like her, depressed. He says of himself,

> I feed too much on inward sources; I live too much with the dead. My mind is something like a ghost of an ancient, wandering about the world and trying mentally to construct it as it used to be, in spite of ruin and confusing changes. (p.40)

While he is apparently talking about his researches, there could hardly be a better account of a depleted inner world of lost objects which he is seeking to recover and restore.

But for Casaubon too, the wish to be in touch with life rather than death appears in his reflection about marriage: he was, 'determined to abandon himself to a stream of feeling, and perhaps was surprised what an exceedingly shallow rill it was.' (p.87) With the beginnings of insight he wonders if Dorothea might also be suffering from some deficiency which was failing to wake a more powerful desire in himself. Intimation of these feelings is also hinted in his reflection on the approaching marriage:

> . . . as the day fixed for his marriage came nearer, Mr Casaubon did not find his spirits rising; nor did the contemplation of that matrimonial garden-scene, where, as all experience showed, the path was to be bordered with flowers, prove persistently more enchanting to him than the accustomed vaults where he walked taper in hand. He did not confess to himself, still less could he have breathed to another, his surprise that though he had won a lovely and noble-hearted girl he had not won delight. (p.111)

There can scarcely be a more delicate expression of the conflict between the faintly stirring wish for delight and its repression in 'the accustomed vaults where he walked taper in hand'.

Although we learn little or nothing about Casaubon's early life, one interesting matter is disclosed. He is an only child, and his mother's sister made an unfortunate love marriage, as a result of which she was denied any share of the family estate. Casaubon, although deeply conventional, had taken it upon himself to remedy this situation by making an allowance to his cousins from his own inheritance, and kept a picture of his disgraced aunt Julia alongside the picture of his mother. This can be regarded as indicating some element of displacement of his disowned passionate feelings. The hanging of his aunt's and his mother's picture side by side, together with the total absence of any reference to his father, might also indicate that what was being displaced was an Oedipal, incestuous wish.

In choosing each other, Casaubon and Dorothea seem to have opted to repress sexuality, deny sensuality, and maintain a defensive asceticism – even if unconsciously there might have been a wish to overcome the repression by contacting the unavailable parent represented by the chosen partner. Certainly, Dorothea thought of marriage as being like having a father who would be above her in judgement and knowledge: 'marriage is a state of higher duties. I never thought of it as mere personal ease.' (p.64)

Even before the marriage has occurred, we are made aware that Dorothea's repression is already weakening. Ladislaw, Casaubon's second cousin and grandson of the wayward aunt Julia, is discovered sketching in the grounds of Casaubon's house, and is introduced to Dorothea, her sister and uncle. As they are introduced,

> Dorothea could see a pair of grey eyes rather near together, a delicate irregular nose with a little ripple in it, and hair falling backward; but there was a mouth and chin of a more prominent threatening aspect than belonged to the type of the grandmother's miniature. (p.104)

Later, walking back to the house leaving Ladislaw to his sketching, Dorothea makes a very kindly reference to him when his character is being traduced by Casaubon. Celia notices and remarks, when the two women are alone, that being engaged to be married seems to have made Dorothea more tolerant. There is a suggestion, then, that what is being repressed is beginning to stir.

The wedding of Dorothea and Casaubon takes place and they honeymoon in Rome so that Casaubon can consult the Vatican archives for material for his lifelong research, 'The Key to all Mythologies'. This involves much time being spent away from Dorothea. Ladislaw makes an appearance in Rome, as if to represent the repressed now displaced, outside the boundary of the couple relationship. Under the emotional turmoil that the Roman antiquities create in her, coupled with the neglect by her husband and a renewed communication with Ladislaw, Dorothea becomes aware of a growing disillusionment with Casaubon, not only for his inability to be in touch with their shared, repressed sensuality, but also with his intellectual accomplishments, which she is beginning to question and despise, although they had originally formed an important part of her choice of him.

'Having once embarked on your marital voyage,' Eliot comments, 'it is impossible not to be aware that you make no way and that the sea is not in sight – that, in fact, you are exploring an enclosed basin.' (p.228) The basin, representing the marriage, was not only enclosed but becalmed, and, as the exchanges between Casaubon and Dorothea in Rome make clear, it was not available to be disturbed by the stirring currents of sensuality newly aroused in Dorothea. Small wonder, then, that her dormant sensuality should begin to respond unwittingly to Ladislaw's presence.

Eliot makes it clear that the growing conflict in Dorothea was echoed in Casaubon, although with less hope of happy resolution. His wish for joy was hemmed in by the habits of 50 years, where he was 'present at the great spectacle of life' and could 'never be liberated from a small hungry shivering self – never . . . be fully possessed by the glory' he beheld. (p.314)

On their return from Rome, Eliot indicates that Dorothea is already changing psychologically and is becoming aware of her repressed wishes. The conflict is eloquently expressed:

Marriage . . . had not yet freed her from the gentlewoman's oppressive liberty; it had not even filled her leisure with ruminant joy of unchecked tenderness. Her blossoming full-pulsed youth stood there in a moral imprisonment which made itself one with the chill, colourless, narrowed landscape, with the shrunken furniture, the never-read books, and the ghostly stag in a pale fantastic world that seemed to be vanishing from daylight. (pp.307–8)

The contrast between her beginning-to-bloom inner world and Casaubon's shrivelled condition is starkly conveyed. He is already suffering from palpitations, which herald a full heart attack precipitated by the receipt of a letter to Dorothea from Ladislaw. The somaticization of the emotional conflict within Casaubon could hardly be better signified than through a failure of the organ conventionally symbolizing the seat of the emotions.

Although Casaubon recovers from the first heart attack, its immediate cause – the intrusion of the denied sensuality in the shape of Ladislaw – is presented and represented again and again as occasions for meetings and communications between him and Dorothea arise. Casaubon's anxiety continues to grow as he perceives the developing sensuality in Dorothea and her responsiveness to Ladislaw. He feels sure that Dorothea has caused both Ladislaw's return from Rome and his determination to remain at Middlemarch against his wishes. He is disturbed by her suggestion that Ladislaw be included in his will to rectify past injustices suffered by that side of the family. 'It was as clear as possible', he believed, 'that she was ready to be attached to Will (Ladislaw) and to be pliant to his suggestions.' (p.457) This implies that the inner struggle against the repressed that each brought to the marriage has now been split so that Casaubon becomes the repressing force and Dorothea expresses the repressed. The internal conflict within each of them becomes an external one between them. To some extent, to accommodate herself to Casaubon's repressive wishes, Dorothea displaces the repressed on to Ladislaw, whose impulsive, emotional character makes him an appropriate target for the displacement. The conflict between Casaubon and Dorothea then becomes one between Casaubon and Ladislaw. It does not, however, cease to exist within and between Casaubon and Dorothea.

Following Casaubon's consultation with his doctor about his health, Eliot writes of his mental turmoil as he contemplates the possibility of death. In that condition he is met by Dorothea in the garden, but is unable to respond to her ardent wish to comfort him. Neither can reach the other:

> . . . it is in these acts called trivialities [Eliot comments] that the seeds of joy are for ever wasted, until men and women look around with haggard faces at the devastation their own waste has made, and say, the earth bears no harvest of sweetness – calling their denial knowledge. (p.462)

In a scene in church, when all three are present, at the height of the conflict between them, Casaubon robs the marriage of hope by his rebuff of Ladislaw and, by implication, of Dorothea's wish to bring into the marriage the sensuality represented by him. The screw tightens as Casaubon asks her to promise that in the event of his death she will comply with a desire he does not specify. In turmoil, Dorothea refuses to make such a promise in ignorance, but agrees to give him her answer in the morning. The conflict in Casaubon is evidently too great, and he dies from a further heart attack in the garden, waiting for Dorothea's reply. Such was his anxiety that he had made a codicil to his will denying her his estate if she married Ladislaw. In the end, even his identification with his passionate aunt is disowned. By threatening to disinherit Dorothea, he identifies with his grandfather and deals with his errant feelings in the same controlling way.

The marriage ends without resolving the unconscious emotional conflict which Casaubon and Dorothea had brought to it. Dorothea's story has not ended, however, and although at first she makes an attempt to continue her husband's life work, she soon gives it up. While knowing nothing of the codicil to Casaubon's will, she begins to react to Ladislaw in a romantic way. Yet she does not recognize her feelings for him, and tells Celia that she will never remarry, and that she intends to devote her life to good works.

Ladislaw does not know of the codicil either, but learns of it by chance some weeks later while he is still in Middlemarch. He then plans to leave, but not before a final meeting with Dorothea. She then becomes fully conscious of her love for him and recognizes that this has been the case since their meeting in Rome. She makes an attempt to sublimate her feelings through study (adopting the defence represented by her marriage to Casaubon), but this fails even before Ladislaw makes another appearance. They meet while a storm rages outside, although within they are having a calm and rather stilted conversation. A flash of lightning and a crack of thunder breaks the spell and they fall into each other's arms. But it is as if the final triumph of the repressed is to be denied until Dorothea can voluntarily renounce Casuabon's estate, determining to live with Ladislaw on her own income and thereby symbolically asserting her separate self, and the integration of her sensuality with her asceticism.

Soames and Irene[3]

The story of Soames and Irene is set some 50 years later than that of Dorothea and Casaubon, whose courtship and marriage lasted only a couple of years. When Soames and Irene are first mentioned they have been married three years and the marriage is already in difficulties. The members of the Forsyte family are very aware of and disturbed by the problem since it seems to threaten the established order. Although the social world of *Middlemarch* is in evidence in the story of Dorothea and Casaubon, it appears much less oppressive than for the Forsytes in the closing years of the nineteenth century.

The story of Soames and Irene is told from the point of view of Soames, while Irene is observed from the outside. She is depicted more enigmatically than Soames, whose inner conflict is much more starkly and dramatically conveyed. He was the first-born of his parents, and although nothing is told directly of his upbringing, something of it is represented in the prevailing preoccupations of the family members: they are intensely interested in money and possessions, and the price of something is an important element in its enjoyment.

Soames has become a partner in the family firm of solicitors, and is already a 'man of property', a most important attribute among the Forsytes. He is presented as being meticulous over his appearance: it was 'impossible to conceive him with a hair out of place, a tie deviating one eighth of an inch from the perpendicular, a collar unglossed'. (pp.68–9) In addition to this very 'buttoned-up' appearance, he is concerned with possessions and possessing. He collects pictures which he keeps with their faces to the wall in a room in his London house; evidently, what was on their backs was as important to him as what was on their fronts, and attested to the only thing he valued – the price which they might command. Even Irene was like a piece of property to be compared with 'this dining table with its deep tints, the starry soft-petalled roses, the ruby-coloured glass, and quaint silver furnishing; could a man own anything prettier than the woman who sat at it'. (p.70)

This presentation was not the whole story, for beneath that conventional, conforming surface lay a turmoil of conflicting desires and feelings. Soames felt an intense longing for Irene herself, and for a period of two years before they married he pursued her passionately and determinedly. She refused him again and again until, 'adroitly taking advantage of an acute phase of her dislike of her home surroundings he crowned his labours with success'. (p.59) When he was in company with her at family or other events, 'he was seldom far from Irene's side . . . and even when separated by the exigencies of social intercourse, could be seen following her about with his eyes in which were strange expressions of watchfulness and longing'. (p.17) Some of this longing was reflected in his relationship with his property: '. . . out of all the things he had collected, his silver, his pictures, his houses, his investments, he got a secret and intimate feeling: from her he got none'. (p.70)

Here it seems to be suggested that his wish for intimacy has been sublimated and reinvested in inanimate objects which he could possess and control without the possibility of loss, and that Irene, whom he could not own in the same way, exposed an unbearable vulnerability in him which hindered his desired intimacy with her. His thoughts at the dinner table, when she is silent and abstracted are perhaps indicative of that vulnerability. He wants to tell her about his decision to build her a house in the country but feels nervous and irritated about it: '. . . she had no business to make him feel like that – a wife and a husband being one person'. (p.70) His aching wish for a symbiotic tie with her is unbearable, especially as he is aware, in company with all the Forsytes that Irene no longer wishes to share his bedroom.

Little or nothing appears explicitly in the novel to explain the origins of this painful conflict in Soames, but it is noticeable that his mother scarcely makes an appearance, and is often absent from family gatherings. Her response to the news of Irene's later abandonment of Soames, while affectionate, is scarcely effusive. And her relationship with James, her husband, seems less than intimate. When James' elder sister Ann dies, 'of all the brothers and sisters James manifested the most emotion. Tears rolled down the parallel furrows of his thin face; where could he go now to tell his troubles he did not know.' (p.102) Not, evidently, to his wife, the mother of Soames.

Perhaps what is being indicated is that Soames' relationship with his mother is as detached as that of his father. This may have given rise to an intense and sublimated wish for symbiotic closeness, which cannot be easily consummated. Such closeness with an animate rather than an inanimate object incurred the prospect of loss, as Soames was discovering with Irene.

At first sight, Irene seemed to be somebody who might be able to provide what Soames was seeking; a free spirit through whom he could recover his own repressed wishes and enjoy the unity for which he longed. She was capable of inspiring affection and 'men were attracted by her; their looks, manners, voices betrayed it; . . . she was one of those women . . . born to be loved and to love, who, when not loving, are not living . . .' (p.59) It is possible to understand Soames's longing for and wish to marry her as an attempt to abate the painful feelings of deprivation resulting from the cool detachment of his mother. It is often the case that when the opposite of early experience is sought and apparently found, what is discovered is that the original detached object lies beneath.

It is more difficult to understand Irene's motives for marrying Soames. She plainly did not wish to do so, and found him physically repulsive, although Soames was in the eyes of the world, and of the Forsytes in particular, a very desirable catch; Irene came from a poor family and had no surviving parent apart from her stepmother, with whom it is hinted she was not on good terms. What the death of her mother, and subsequently of her father after his remarriage, may have meant to her is not described. The somewhat teasing quality of her interactions with men, and her powerful resistance to Soames may suggest that she had an anxiety about intimacy which meshed with Soames' inability to be intimate with any woman. In the light of subsequent events in the marriage, it might be speculated that she was made anxious by the powerful sexual reactions she so readily provoked in men and was looking for someone whose strong defensive system would help her to manage her own potentially dangerous sexuality. With Soames, however, she became more estranged from and threatened by those feelings.

The marriage is in difficulties from the outset, and neither Soames nor the family can understand why. Soames reflects upon his virtues as a husband and cannot understand what she might find wrong with him: 'It was not as if he drank! Did he run into debt, or gamble, or swear; was he violent; were his friends rackety; did he stay out at night?' (p.58) What he was unable to conceive was that the 'subdued aversion' to him that he was aware of might be a result of his unexpressed passion and unconscious emotional withdrawal, expressed through listing as his virtues what he was not, rather than what he was.

Just before the dramatic crisis in their marriage they are at a dance given by one of the elder Forsytes. Soames, 'danced with no one. Some fellows danced with their wives: his sense of "form" had never permitted him to dance with Irene *since their marriage*.' (p.182; my italics) It might be wondered if in marriage he was now repeating the cool relationship with his mother and unconsciously punishing her in Irene. Such repetitions regularly occur in marriages where each of the partners may be seeking to repeat and repair something from earlier relationships with parents.

Into such a relationship, which has become stuck for both partners and where the possibilities of escape seem blocked, a third party may intervene, representing the missing or repressed elements in it and bringing matters to a head. Such a person is Bosinney, an artistically-minded architect, who is engaged to Irene's close friend, June Forsyte. His artistic temperament and lack of business qualities are regarded with great suspicion by the Forsytes. Irene and Bosinney make an immediate rapport.

Interestingly, Soames decides that he will engage Bosinney, despite his reputation, to design and build a house for him in the country with the intention of moving to live there with Irene, and the hope that it will improve the marriage. It is as if he unconsciously apprehends what is missing and that it might be something represented by Bosinney. Equally interesting is that he finds the remedy rapidly begins to cost him more than he can afford, and perhaps not only in economic terms. The persistent failure of Bosinney to observe cost constraints drives Soames to rage, in which jealousy about the relationship between Irene and Bosinney is combined with fury about Bosinney's prodigality. His proposal to take punitive action against Bosinney, (which may have precipitated Bosinney's subsequent death in a road accident), and his threats to make him bankrupt, succeed in estranging Irene from himself. She locks her bedroom door against him and refuses to relent. The stalemate endures until one night Soames discovers that she has failed to lock her door. He enters and rapes her, dealing with his subsequent guilty feelings by regarding it as 'the first step towards reconciliation', and as doing his best 'to sustain the sanctity of marriage, to prevent her from abandoning her duty'. (p.265)

The marriage of Soames and Irene ends after a 12-year separation, when Soames decides he wants a divorce to be able to marry a young French woman, Annette. He discovers, as he tries to open the possibility of divorce, that he is still emotionally embroiled with Irene. He makes unsuccessful attempts to persuade or force her to return. He marries Annette, but equally fails to solve his emotional problems with her. This brief scene which takes place after the birth of their daughter epitomizes the whole of his difficulty:

> Annette was very pale and very pretty lying there. The baby was hidden away somewhere: he could not see it. He went up to the bed, and with sudden emotion bent and kissed her forehead.

'Here you are then, Soames,' she said. 'I am not so bad now. But I suffered terribly, terribly. I am glad I cannot have any more. Oh! how I suffered.'

Soames stood silent, stroking her hand; words of endearment, of sympathy, absolutely would not come; the thought passed through him: 'An English girl wouldn't have said that!' At this moment he knew with certainty he would never be near to her in spirit and in truth, nor she to him. He had collected her – that was all! (p.631)

He never rids himself of the intensity of his frustrated passion for Irene, and at the end of the book he sits in Highgate cemetery after a family funeral reflecting on his life:

> And only one thing really troubled him, sitting there – the melancholy craving in his heart – because the sun was like enchantment on his face and on the clouds and on the golden birch leaves, and the wind's rustle was so gentle, and the yew trees green and dark, and the sickle moon so pale in the sky. He might wish and wish and never get it – the beauty and the loving in the world. (p.906)

If Soames had been unable to resolve his problems satisfactorily, Irene is eventually more successful in finding ways of dealing with hers. The unleashing of sexual destructiveness, brought about in her marriage and in her relationship with Bosinney, leads her to withdraw from life for many years. Her sexuality is sublimated in work with prostitutes.

In the meantime, Soames' uncle, Old Jolyon, decides to leave her sufficient money in trust so that she will have a comfortable income for the rest of her life after he dies. His son, Young Jolyon (so-called although he is in his early 50's) is to be her trustee, and becomes her confidant. Soames, having with difficulty decided on remarriage, has to obtain evidence of Irene's adultery, although she has been living perfectly chastely for the 12 years they have lived apart. He sets a detective to watch Irene, who reports that she has been frequently visited by Young Jolyon. Soames, although he is aware of the trustee relationship, cannot believe that they are not also having a sexual relationship. He visits them unexpectedly at Robin Hill, where they have been served with divorce papers naming Young Jolyon as correspondent. Although it is made clear by Galsworthy that the relationship is chaste, confronted by Soames in person they agree that they are living together. This leads them to give effect to that admission by going away to Europe together. After the divorce they marry and have a son.

For Irene this can be seen as an integration of all aspects of her personality in a relationship, and a resolution of the conflict about sexuality within herself which has been either destructive or repressed. Young Jolyon is himself an artist, who in his youth left his first wife and daughter to take a lover with whom he had two more children. He was not concerned with the all-consuming passion of the Forsytes for property, but after his first wife's death he was reconciled with his father and rejoined the family without giving up his artistic career. So he can be seen as a man who has reconciled, within himself, an unruly passionate nature with the requirements of society without loss of integrity, and who is therefore available for Irene to help her with similar conflicts and the task of defusing the destructive aspects of her sexuality. It is symbolic of this that the couple live together in the beautiful house completed by Bosinney before his death, as if something of that artistic passion can now be a container of rather than the catalyst for destructive forces.

A further inexplicable aspect of this integration (but one which points towards an Oedipal complexity in Irene which is never clarified in the story), is that Irene has married the father of her friend, June, whose lover, Bosinney, she had seduced. Furthermore, they live together in the house built for her by Bosinney, which had been bought by her husband's father who made the legacy which had released her from financial dependency on Soames. This perhaps hints at a much deeper conflict than Galsworthy has been able to make explicit in the story, but which he has somehow tied off rather neatly in this outcome.

The authors of these two accounts of marriage wrote in the second half of the nineteenth century and in the first quarter of the twentieth century, each setting their stories in an earlier time period. Despite this, the marriages they describe could in terms of their emotional content, be set in any period. It is especially interesting that each of the women find the resolution of their problems in a second marriage rather than the first. The ready availability of divorce in the final third of the twentieth century inclines us to regard this as a particularly modern solution to conflict in marriage, but here are two authors, writing at different times, considering remarriage as a way in which problems of earlier relationships can be healthily resolved. Galsworthy contrasts this with what he thought was the general view of the late Victorians, that even when the marriage was unsatisfactory the partners '. . . should jog along, even if they hated each other. It would not matter if they went their own ways a little so long as the decencies were observed – the sanctity of the marriage tie, of the common home, respected.' (p.205) This opinion is not too far from the position of some modern moralists, although they would be unlikely to express their view so bluntly; for them it is the form rather than the content of marriage that is important.

It is a view of commitment that contrasts starkly with the basic theme of the marriage of Soames and Irene where not only were the decencies disregarded, but also where Soames' wish to reassert appearances, as he conceived them, resulted in a violent rape and the complete rupture of the relationship. Does this not resemble outcomes of contemporary relationships in which one partner feels driven to act violently, sometimes as an attempt to re-establish the bond and sometimes to break it finally?

It is easy to see in the account of these two marriages the same sense as is often found in modern marriages of one of the two partners being the victim of the other. In some respects both partners can be thought of as being the victim of the other. The two women are presented much more sympathetically than either of their husbands, and in the first instance may be seen as the victims of rather insensitive, repressed men. However, the husbands clearly thought of themselves as the victims when the third party, in the shape of the liberated artist who was the antithesis of each of them, appeared on the scene. But what is evident from the accounts is that these situations were choices made consciously and unconsciously by each of the partners.

For both authors, as for modern marital therapists and counsellors, marriage can be understood as a container within which conflicting emotions and unresolved problems and legacies of past relationships may be held while solutions are attempted (Clulow, 1985; Colman, 1993; Jung, 1925; Morley, 1984; Pincus, 1973). The relationship incorporates for both partners unresolved issues from the past with the prospect of reworking them anew, so that anxiety-arousing conflicts may be creatively managed.

For Dorothea and Casaubon, and for Soames and Irene, what is ambivalently warded off is dangerous sensuality and sexuality. Dorothea and Casaubon have each displaced their sexuality, although for different reasons which have not been made explicit in their story. Dorothea has displaced hers on to her sister; Casaubon has displaced his on to a disgraced aunt, perhaps as a safer object of his Oedipal sexual love than his mother. As with all couples, the hope exists that the displaced or repressed aspects of the partners may be found in their 'other half', and kept safely distant but within the boundaries of the marriage (see Chapter 4).

The ambivalent struggle of Soames and Irene with violent and passionate wishes is evident throughout the story, even to the last page of the book. In the presence of a passionate woman, Soames' needs remain repressed and frustrated, subdued by anal preoccupations with possessions and collecting. It is as if his powerful sexual wishes, related to the desire for unification with the mother and its expression in the wish for a symbiotic marriage, are feared because of their potential destructive and incestuous nature, and, in the incident of the rape of Irene, their actual destructiveness.

That Irene's sexuality is held equally ambivalently, despite her apparent ease with herself, is conveyed in the choice of the undemonstrative but repressed Soames, and his capacity to control the outward expression of passion. He contrasts with the many other men who are immediately attracted to Irene, and who would have offered a more satisfactory choice if she was really as comfortable with her sexuality as she appears to be. Moreover, that she shared at an unconscious level Soames' fear of the destructiveness of her sexual passion is demonstrated by her reaction to what happened after she allowed it to be unleashed with her lover, Bosinney. The violent death is followed by her complete withdrawal from sexual relationships during the 12-year separation from Soames.

Both couples, in different ways and for different reasons, are ambivalently concerned with sensuality and sexuality, as are many twentieth century couples, despite the greater sexual openness of our time. In choosing each other partners are looking not only for help to express aspects of themselves about which they feel fearful, but also, because of the anxiety created by the threat of raising repressed wishes to consciousness, they are seeking support to maintain the repression in the partnership. In this, our fictitious couples are no different from many modern couples who cannot gain with each other the intimate gratification that is both sought and feared.

As with other couples, there are aspects of unconscious phantasy which are shared (Bannister and Pincus, 1965; Teruel, 1966). The evident depression of both Dorothea and Casaubon suggest the possibility of their being unconsciously preoccupied with similar object relations. Although conjectural, the absence of any real reference to either of their fathers, and the possibility that Dorothea is in a state of uncompleted mourning for her father, may mean that they have in common a shared preoccupation with the loss of a male internal object relevant to their anxiety about the expression of sexuality. Similarly, Soames and Irene may have in common a preoccupation with the lack of a gratifying maternal figure. For Soames at least, Irene embodies the distant, unobtainable woman who frustrates intimate contact and threatens abandonment. For Irene, a dead mother has been replaced by a stepmother with whom it is hinted she is conflict. Might she have had some feeling about the loss of her own mother which resonated with Soames' striving to unite with his remote mother? The loss of her mother might have been experienced first with guilt, because of her Oedipal relationship with father, and then with fury when he remarries. In that case, the unconscious fury about father's betrayal might easily be displaced on to Soames. Her marriage to Young Jolyon appears to provide a resolution to the Oedipal conflict, and perhaps a triumphant entry into the role of the envied stepmother.

Finally, the introduction of a third party is a common feature of many marriages, and may be seen as an attempt to deal with an ambivalent aspect of the marriage by displacing it outside its boundary. The intervening person may be seen to represent the desired but feared elements of the relationship which cannot be contained within it. Both Bosinney and Ladislaw represent an easy sensuality and emotional availability which is missing from both marriages. Soames, in engaging Bosinney to build a house for himself and Irene, seems to be seeking to possess some of Bosinney's emotional availability and to incorporate it in bricks and mortar, as if it will then somehow, become part of the marriage. He can afford neither the economic price nor the emotional cost of this manoeuvre, and so it ends in disaster and the complete breakdown of his relationship with Irene.[4]

Ladislaw, because of the blood relationship and the fact that he is the grandson of Casaubon's sexually free aunt, is an ideal target for displaced and disowned sexuality. For both Dorothea and Casaubon he represents what is missed and feared in the marriage, and his family links make the return of the repressed even more threatening, leading to Casaubon's repeatedly vain attempts to force him to leave Middlemarch. As we have seen, Dorothea is less fearful, and attempts to bring him into relation with the marriage through her wish that Casaubon restore the inheritance lost to him, and her silent hope that his presence can be accepted and acknowledged. Casaubon's very weak wish for sexual gratification in the marriage cannot sustain even its symbolic realization in Ladislaw's intrusion across the boundary, however platonically. His response is to try and expel the threat and reinforce the sublimation of his sexuality in his work.

In these two marriages, set in widely different historical periods both relatively remote from our own and in different social classes, there can be seen many of the elements which continue to appear in contemporary marriages. Like Dorothea and Casaubon, Soames and Irene, we also choose partners who bring to the relationship psychological conflicts which mesh with our own, and which offer opportunities to find new and gratifying resolutions. As with them, where defences against the repressed material are too great the relationship will fail, but like them, many will seek to find a solution with another who may offer greater hope of a successful outcome. However we interpret the meanings, what is clearly demonstrated is that the intimate nature of relationships and the problems they are attempting to solve remain unchanged whatever the fluctuations in social condition and moral climate. The difficulties of couples in an earlier century may not have been so different from those facing couples in our own time.

Robert Morley

Notes

1   All references are from the Penguin English Library edition, ed. W. J. Harvey, 1982.
2   It is interesting here that although Dorothea may be regarded as a 'new woman', her motivation is religious.
3   All references are from Penguin Books Edition, 1978.
4   Soames' longing is transferred to his daughter, Fleur, who falls in love with Irene's and Jolyon's son, Jon. The possibility of that relationship revives memories of painful unresolved conflicts. Irene is particularly unable to allow even the vicarious forgiveness of the past which would have been represented by the marriage of their two children.

7
Sexual Revolutions

The image of a married couple, smiles a little forced, bodies pulling apart even as hands are entwined, with a caption reading: 'Politician's wife says, "I'm standing by him," ' is so common as scarcely to seem newsworthy. And yet, newsworthy it is. Stories of the sexual infidelities of powerful men continue to pull readers from someone else's newspaper to the one with the picture and the story. By contrast, rarely do we see the same image with the caption, 'Politician's husband says, "I'm standing by her." ' And if we did, would readers be attracted in the same way?

While little has changed in the condemnation of the 'other woman', 'mistress' or 'bimbo', it is comparatively recently that public male figures have lost their jobs or been exposed as a result of their sexual infidelities. An image of marriage is formed:

- the committed, especially the married, couple, remains ideally in a sexually exclusive relationship;
- powerful men, none the less, take mistresses or have affairs;
- good wives forgive their husbands' affairs, even when these men have fathered a child by the 'other woman';
- such affairs are not really the man's fault but that of the 'other woman', or perhaps of the not good-enough wife;
- when men are caught breaking private rules while holding public office they may be expected to do public penance for private shame by resigning their jobs (usually, there is no longer the pretence of a security risk – the tale that used to be told).
- while women, including wives, can no longer be safely placed in categorical boxes (whore, virgin, clone) they are still expected to play a heavily supportive role.

In the Western world, similar stories recur in each generation in slightly altered form, indicating a deep and powerful desire for erotic and passionate relationships and reflecting what is happening to gender relations. I give them the status of myths or mythologies – not to indicate any untruth, but to suggest their power to act as guiding narratives for our everyday (and sometimes newsworthy) lives. *David and Bathsheba*, *Tristan and Isolde*, *Anna Karenina*, *Fatal Attraction*, all describe the love triangle: a man or woman married or bound to another and the interloping third who feels desire, and for whom desire is felt so strongly that social convention, normal roles, maternal or paternal duty, filial obligation, honour and shame become negotiable – albeit only with danger. The outcome of these tales is no light matter. In most, the lover or mistress (or both), must die. In particular, it is the other woman or the straying wife who cannot be allowed to live.

What, if anything, has changed to indicate a sexual revolution or revolutions? Commentators and scholars argue that evidence is lacking for even one revolution. Feminists, especially, ask, 'What revolution?' and, 'Whose revolution?' The trend towards, for example, more premarital sex was evident well before the mid-1960s to mid-1970s when the sexual liberation of women and of gay people is usually placed. But revolutions are made of more than statistics. Revolutions are made of attitudes and beliefs, ideologies and mythologies, narratives and scripts that enable and perhaps even cause change. Together with the acceleration of pre-existing trends in sexual behaviour before the late 1960s and early 1970s, there has been a shift in attitudes sufficiently profound to speak of a revolution. A revolution, if not for men, for women and for gay people.

Revolutions may not be successful; they may meet no one's ideals or only those of some, generally those who take power. Often revolution is followed by a backlash, and changes that at first appear liberating turn out to constrain people in unexpected ways. Women have noted they were granted the freedom to say, 'yes', in accordance with male desire, but there has been less freedom to articulate their own scripts, their own patterns of desire.

In this chapter I first examine figures and feelings. How many do what and how do they feel about it now as compared with, say, a generation ago? Next, I expand on those feelings by looking at the expectations women and men bring to marriage and what processes might lead to having an affair, to 'committing adultery'. This section ties modern marriage to ancient myths, to legends about adultery and the nature of erotic and caring love which offer narratives that are still immensely influential. Finally, by using a case history, I suggest a way links may be forged between public and private contracts, between the acknowledged, known about scripts or narratives of marriage, and those secret ones of which we may be unaware (see Chapter 4).

Revolutions

Abandoning Virginity

Until the 1960s in the UK, despite the 'flapping' 1920s and the consequences of world wars, it was not unusual for young people to regard their virginity as a prize, something special that was to be 'saved' for marriage. This was not restricted to the religious or even just to women; some men, too, prized virginity in themselves. Virginity was motivated, but not controlled, by fear of pregnancy. Despite commentators linking the contraceptive pill to massive increases in premarital sexual behaviour, figures show this increasing rapidly before the pill was widely available.

A recent survey of sexual behaviour in Britain showed that both women and men now experience first intercourse, on average, at 17 years of age (Wellings et al., 1994). This is a full four years earlier for women and three for men than for the oldest groups in the study who were aged 45 to 59 in 1990 (when the study was conducted). It was the 1950s – the decade in which women born between 1931 and 1941 were first having sex, on average at an earlier age than their older sisters – that witnessed the biggest and fastest drop in age. Although the pill was introduced in 1961, it was not widely available until later;

Table 7: Marital Status and First Intercourse

	WOMEN		MEN	
Age:	45–49	16–24	45–49	16–24
	Cumulative Percentages			
Married	39	1	14	
Engaged	52	4	20	1
Cohabiting		5		
Going steady	86	68	57	49
	Percentages by Category			
Known sexual partner	12	23	25	30
Met recently	1	7	11	17
Just met – range:	1–2		4–5	

Source: Wellings, Kaye et al.: Sexual Behaviour in Britain, London: Penguin, 1994.

in practice, it was not available to unmarried women until 1972 and to those unable to pay until 1975.

It is not only that women and men are first having sex earlier than their mothers and fathers, but also that the oldest group surveyed (aged 45 to 59) differ hugely from the youngest (16 to 24) in the *circumstances* of first intercourse (see Table 7).

The oldest and youngest women had their first experience of sexual intercourse in a relationship of some duration and meaning more frequently than either the oldest or youngest men. The change in choice of circumstance is the same for both sexes, but much more dramatic and marked for women: whereas compared with their elders young men were twice as likely to have first sex with a known but not steady partner, or one met very recently, young women were seven times more likely to do so. Why are women behaving more like men?

Convergence between women and men

To answer this question, we need to ask why the pill was invented, manufactured, advertised, made readily available, and, more importantly still, taken up by millions of women just when it was – in the mid-1960s and 1970s. Perhaps women had decided that saving themselves for marriage was not such a great idea? But illegitimacy was still an appalling stigma in people's lives; *if* the father was known and could be persuaded, the young couple were coerced into marriage. Otherwise, young women could be sent away; some were removed to asylums for having dared to have sex and given birth to an illegitimate child. Women certainly did not want babies unless they were married. Perhaps it is that they felt, in increasing numbers, that they had some entitlement to behave rather more as men did.

One of the most discernible trends is, indeed, a *convergence* between women and men in behaviour, and, perhaps even in feelings. Now, with women and men first having intercourse at about the same age, it is outmoded even to use the phrase 'premarital sex', although there remains a distinction in the kinds of relationships women seem to prefer: relationships of some duration and commitment. Although the overall proportions of people who are cohabiting in a couple state is still low, it is rising fast (see Chapter 1), especially among young adults – those aged between 20 and 34. Nearly one-third of babies nowadays are born to women who are not married and of these, three-quarters are registered in both parents' names, many of whom will be living together. The couple state, according to McRae's (1993) study of cohabiting mothers, shares many features with, but does not precisely mirror, the marital relationship. In particular, it may be less durable. As yet, we are not able to tell what proportions will eventually marry, so we cannot know whether these relationships are *pre*-marital or *non*-marital. But the change is significant. In the period before the mid-1970s, numerous articles assessed the psychopathology of women who had premarital sex. It was deviant behaviour. Women who did that sort of thing were in need of psychological help; they were not just women with healthy appetites (women's appetites are a problem not only to men but to women themselves: sex and food are but the most obvious examples of conflict). Recent changes in patterns of and attitudes towards premarital sex can surely be termed revolutionary.

Homosexuality

Leaving prevalence to one side, Wellings' survey of sexual behaviour found a clear pattern of convergence between men and women over homosexuality. The greatest discrepancy between women and men in reporting having had a same-sex partner was in the oldest, and the least discrepancy in the youngest age group. What is clear, however, is that while women may make a homosexual debut at any age and after years of heterosexual experience, men are much less likely to do so. The life pattern is quite diverse. Women who are considerably more likely to have had a female partner are those who have many *male* partners. Perhaps they are women whose very sexual quest lies in an unhappiness with the mould into which they have been pressed from birth. And, if we think about our ageing population, with women living as widows or divorcees, it may be that they feel they can only achieve the kind of partnerships they seek with another woman.

In summary, I have touched on four items evidenced by the figures:

- increased sexual activity at earlier ages for both women and men;
- increased homosexual expression among those who have many partners of the opposite sex;
- increased similarity or convergence of experience between women and men in heterosexual behaviour;
- continuing preference among women compared with men for sex within stable and meaningful relationships.

Attitudes and Adultery

While there has been a massive change in behaviour relating to premarital or non-married heterosexual sex, accompanied by an equal shift in tolerance of such relationships, there has been no *equivalent* change in extramarital sex and attitudes to it. The sexual revolution appears to relate to early premarital or non-married sex, and to homosexuality .

No one knows how many people have what Wellings and her co-authors call 'concurrent' sexual partners. My review of many studies – from Kinsey in America (1948; 1953) or Gorer (1971) and Schofield (1973) in the UK, to the *Redbook* and various women's magazines – led to the view that for people married at least two years, about 60 per cent of men and 40 per cent of women might be expected to have at least one additional partner in at least one of their marriages (Lawson, 1990). The new survey asked different questions and reported that about 15 per cent of men and 8 per cent of women had had 'concurrent relationships' in the last five years. If the respondent was married, the figures fell to about 10 per cent of men and less than 5 per cent of women. For unexplained reasons the data show cohabitants conforming to the pattern of single rather than married people; approaching 30 per cent of men and 15 per cent of women reported having had more than one partner in the previous five years concurrently with their present cohabitee. Of course, five years is a short time for many marriages, and people may be faithful in one relationship and unfaithful in another. So it is quite possible that over a lifetime, the earlier higher estimates are right.

The study also found, in agreement with all others, that sexual exclusivity remains a powerful ideal for marriage. The rank order for features making for a successful marriage were: faithfulness, mutual respect, sex, having children, shared interests, shared chores, adequate income and shared religious beliefs. There were no differences between women and men. Figure 2 illustrates just how strongly people felt about fidelity and other sexual behaviours, not only in marriage but also in other couple relationships.

The figure also suggests the following conclusions about sexual attitudes:

- only around 10 per cent think premarital sex is always or mostly wrong, and they are mainly in the oldest age groups;
- an overwhelming proportion (80+ per cent) adhere to sexual exclusivity, slightly less to sex outside cohabitation and less again for sex outside a regular partnership;
- women are against one-night stands;
- women are more tolerant of homosexuality than men.

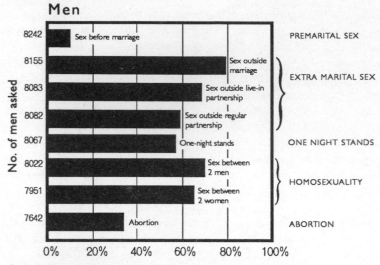

Beliefs that these things are always or mostly wrong

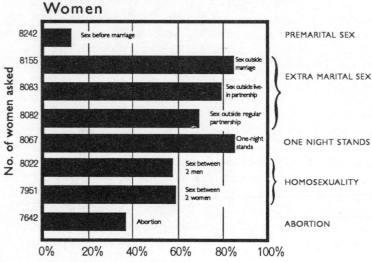

Beliefs that these things are always or mostly wrong

Source: Wellings et al, 1994, p. 236

Figure 2: Attitudes towards sexual behaviour.

Expectations – Marriage and Coupledom

As we have seen, sexual exclusivity plays a central role in the expectations people have of marriage. While like marries like – education, class, colour and intelligence playing a part in people's choices – so does the capacity of the spouse (especially the man) to provide economic security. In McRae's study cohabitees married when the man could offer something financially, and tended not to when he could not.

These external reasons are complemented by the wishes of individuals to have their emotional needs met in a loving relationship. One hope that is born of the sexual revolution – taken in especially but not only by women, if you will, as an emotional need – is for a more egalitarian partnership. This is partially expressed in the 'sharing chores' item listed high by both women and men interviewed in the Wellings survey. At the same time, and born perhaps of the enormous growth industries of psychology, psychotherapy, counselling and other 'talking' professions, there is a desire for 'communication'. Young people say in studies carried out on both sides of the Atlantic, 'I want someone I can really talk to. Someone who will be a friend. Real friends. That you can talk to.' (Sarsby, 1983) This desire is similar for all social classes, races and ethnic minority groups.

Beyond the desire for a good friend and someone who will share what is done at home, women also seek something that has always been part of a man's entitlement: a life in the public as well as the private sphere. Women now rarely have to obtain the permission of men to take a job, and many networks and campaigning organizations strive for women to be visible and participative as equal citizens in all areas of life. Legislation passed during the 1970s against discrimination on the grounds of sex or marital status set the parameters in law for these privately held desires.

The hopes of modern marriage may be encapsulated in two major myths: the *Myth of Romantic Marriage*, and the *Myth of Me* (Lawson, 1990).

The myth of romantic marriage is confused. It contains both the ancient story of adultery about eros (that says passion gives major purpose to life, is an honourable quest, may be felt as much by women as men, is not something that can be controlled, makes the breaching of rules excusable or comprehensible even if it leads to death) and the story about agape (the caring and nurturing love more familiar to the married). Denis de Rougemont (1939) long ago warned that there were no sustaining myths for marriage, only ones for adultery, and that the embracing of adulterous love within the ideal for marital love was bound to bring deep conflict. The conflict lies in the treacherous and usually tragic outcome of eros and the creative, life-enhancing outcomes of agape.

The sexual revolution for women did just that. It brought firmly into the one myth or narrative adventure the idea that passion and marriage went together. Given that people are marrying less, we might rename it the *Myth of Love*. The sexual revolution in its political, liberating sense, brought firm expectations of a partnership that was not about ownership but about sharing, not about women as the property of men (although she usually still is 'given away' by her father and 'taken' by her spouse), but about finding herself in the course of relating to another in an intimate relationship. The woman was now as entitled as her partner to self-fulfilment.

Above all, there was to be a new sharing of thought. If you could not possess another's body you could at least possess their secrets, especially their sexual secrets. In the course of marriage, there is a growth of shared knowledges that we might call the communal knowledge capital of the couple, some of which is also shared with children. This, I think, is what makes the shock of discovery about a spouse's affair so painful, leading to such distressed cries as, 'But I was the last to know! It's not the fact he slept with someone else but the fact they lied; the fact everyone else knew, the fact I didn't know; the fact I was deceived; the fact they know things about me, about us that I thought were private, just for us . . .' The feeling that is less often expressed is that the body has been stolen or given. This sharing, this expectation of equalities in life goals and knowledge suggests a *Myth of Partnership*.

Changes in the myth, reflecting shifts in public belief systems, become part of the unwritten, perhaps unspoken, contract between spouses.

Contracts

Sometimes behaviour and beliefs are so discrepant that there is cognitive dissonance – meaning people cannot adhere to such contradictory beliefs and act the way they do. Although beliefs can alter to fit changes in behaviour, people have to undertake a great deal of emotional labour (Hochshild, 1983) in order to breach the powerful mythologies with which they begin their marital journey, especially as the rules are repeatedly held up to them by the media in examples of failure.

Figure 3 shows that when couples had an agreement to be free, they were; when they assumed they were meant to be faithful, they generally were. Those who were in open relationships often made new rules – for example, that they should be told about their spouse's affairs. So sexual freedom did not release the partners from their contribution to and shared possession of the couple's knowledge capital. The *Myth of Partnership* applied all the more strongly.

But what about the intersection of the public and the private

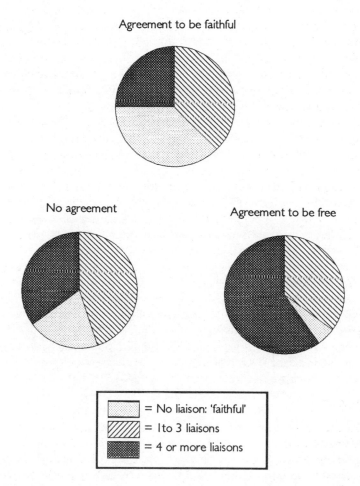

Source: Lawson, *Adultery* p.102

Figure 3: Spouses' agreements and the number of adulterous liaisons.

contract? I have noted that in extramarital sex we cannot trace a sexual revolution parallel to that occurring premaritally. Yet there has been one dramatic change that I call the 'shrinking fidelity span'. This amounts to a greater readiness among younger people, especially younger women, to have an affair earlier in their marriages. This does not necessarily imply more unfaithful people overall, but if you are going to have another sexual partner it is now likely to be sooner rather than later. In my study, the mean number of years of 'waiting' before an affair was nearly nine years for women and eight for men. But, for women married before 1960, the wait was on average 14.5 years; it was eight years if they married in the 1960s and just over four years if they married in the 1970s. Equivalent figures for men are 11, 7.75 and five years. So women have, as it were, overtaken men in the speed with which they have an affair, providing a further example of convergence between women and men's behaviour.

In the talking or telling stakes, there has been a similar convergence, but this time it is men who have changed. Less than half the husbands who had affairs in the earliest period told their wives, but more than three-quarters did so after 1975. (The women discovered the affairs as frequently but from others than their husbands.) Women tell their husbands in around two-thirds of cases, now as in the past. So, there has been a huge increase in men's confessions, overtaking their wives who have hardly changed in this respect. It is as if women have learned to be more like men in the sexual and men more like women in the talking stakes. These shifts, together with others, have led me to describe a masculinization of sex accompanying the feminization of love that others have noted (Cancian, 1986).

A public contract that stresses egalitarianism, openness, communication, sexual equality and non-possession can lead to some unexpected outcomes: for women, what is sauce for the gander can also be sauce for the goose in terms of sexual behaviour; for men, a belief that if he confesses, sharing his secret knowledge with her, she will be forgiving.

I have stressed so far the convergences between women and men. However, there remain differences. Women continue to prefer fewer and more durable encounters which have emotional content for them. They tend to restrict the number of their affairs to between one and three and to insist they are for 'sex'n'friendship', often expressed, as here, in one word; men tend to have between one and five affairs and to say that sex is the outstanding ingredient.

Occupational roles also may introduce differences. Women entering occupations that have been and remain largely male dominated may take on a pattern more typical of men, while men entering

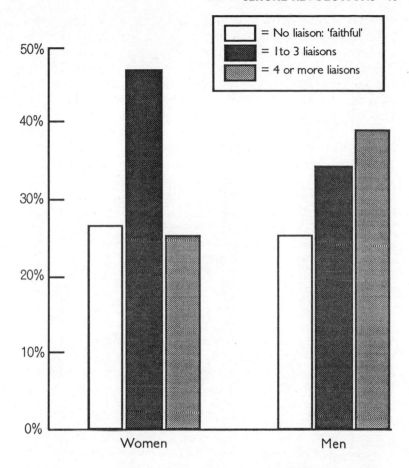

Source: Lawson, *Adultery* p.79

Figure 4: Number of adulterous liaisons for women and men.

occupations that have been and remain female dominated may take on a pattern more typical of women (see Figure 5).

The 'opportunity' argument does not account for these differences, for while it could explain women's increasing adultery in male occupations, it cannot explain men's reduced adultery in female occupations. The concepts of cognitive dissonance and gendered roles are more useful. We can imagine how uncomfortable it may be to work in a setting where every day the importance of caring and communication are held as central values, and simultaneously to be

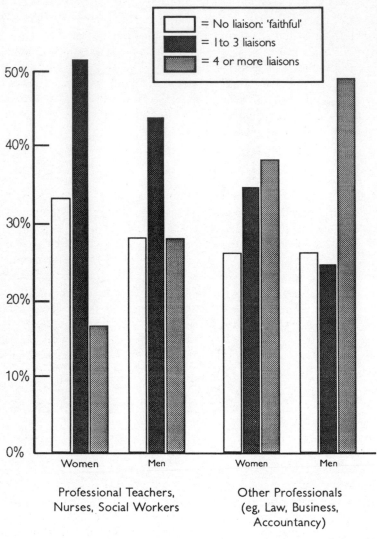

Figure 5: Number of adulterous liaisons, occupational qualifications and sex.

(let us use the word) philandering. Similarly, we can imagine how difficult it might be to work intensively on projects, by both day and night, eating as well as working together, perhaps travelling together, commonly in a fiercely competitive environment, and yet to say 'good-night' at the hotel bedroom door and not have sex. The ethos of male and female-dominated occupations differ. The men or women who cross each other's threshold must become somewhat more feminine (more nurturant), somewhat more masculine (more competitive, thrusting). The conflict, then, arises not because women and men are fundamentally diverse in their desires and responses, but because they are fundamentally affected by the gendered roles they play.

Sophie's Choice

Sophie's story demonstrates the drawing apart of such powerful myths in her marriage. When she married, Sophie felt the chances of developing herself and having a satisfying partnership with Damien were good. When her children were born, she readily gave up work. But this change, together with other major life events, particularly the breakdown of her husband and the death of her mother, left her bereft of support and intellectual companionship. The qualities she needed in her marriage, especially of someone to talk to, were absent in Damien, who was struggling with his business. Furthermore, he seemed to expect what she called 'sexual servicing' that took no account of her needs and feelings. Only when in therapy did they communicate: 'We were closer then than at any time because talking began.' It did not last, and Sophie was tempted by a phone call from an old lover inviting her to lunch. He made her feel the 'assertive, dynamic, imaginative' (his words) person she had been 'up to about two or three years after' her marriage. Sophie said she entered this affair: 'As a housewife and mother. All right, I was doing some freelance art work so I wasn't totally immersed, but I had a very low image at that time . . . Here I was, trapped – kids, nappies, nursery schools, husband who wasn't what I wanted a husband to be, and I was sunk, you know, I was lumbered with it.' (Lawson, 1990: p.134)

If not revolutionary, a decided shift is evident in her determination to settle for nothing less than being able (as she said) to 'move on', 'to do things', to fulfil herself, coupled with a refusal to put up with a less than satisfactory and non-communicative partnership.

Unable to integrate her mythologies, Sophie eventually left the marriage.

Annette Lawson

8
Economic Ties

Money in marriage represents power and control; lack of it limits choices and freedom of action. In this chapter I shall be looking at the economic ties in marriage from the perspective of how the legal rules about sharing resources within marriage fit alongside the ways individuals behave. The socio-economic context of changing family structures, and particularly the economic consequences of divorce for women and children, have been discussed elsewhere (Maclean, 1991). Here, I want to look at the ways resources are shared between adult partners, and between adults and children who may or may not be living in the same household. This can tell us a great deal about how we see these relationships, and how we think about the obligations of family life.

The law reflects and moulds financial relationships within families in response to social, economic and political factors. The 1980s saw the boundaries between family and state obligations being redefined in the UK. As part of the privatization of families, the responsibility for supporting dependent individuals has been firmly redirected towards family members and away from collective or social bodies. The 1991 Child Support Act is a good example of the process, linking as it does financial obligation to biological parenthood. How well are we adapting to the circumstances of our times?

I shall consider the question of money and marriage from three perspectives: the economics of gender; the economics of partnership; and the economics of parenting. In doing so, I shall raise questions about how to square the circle – that is, how to bring about a happier reconciliation of the fact that men do not bear and care for children, and that women do not earn enough to support themselves and their children as is necessary in a society that accepts serial monogamy. The problem is compounded by the rolling back of communal welfare provision for dependants and our failure, despite the start made by the Child Support Agency, to recognize in any effective way the financial responsibilities of parents who do not live with their children.

Money, Men and Women

In developed countries such as those of Western Europe, economic resources consist of earning capacity and entitlement. How do men and women fare respectively in relation to each of these?

Take earning capacity first. In biblical times there were clear inequalities in the relative economic value attached to the labour of women and men. Leviticus 27 lays down that a man shall be valued at 50 shekels of silver and a woman at 30. In a period of equal opportunity in the workplace, underpinned by statute in the UK and supported by European legislation and the International Court of Justice, one might expect that things have changed. Sadly, they have changed very little. Although it is possible to legislate for equal pay for the same work, and to avoid discrimination in hiring procedures, it is *not* possible to dictate who will do which kind of work. The labour market remains highly segregated: it is easy to count the number of male nurses and female doctors, male secretaries and female managers.

Earning capacity includes not only wages and salaries but also the increments, privileges and entitlements to sick-pay and pensions that in our economy go with long term, uninterrupted, full-time employment. Although work patterns are changing, and women are doing well in the growing sectors of service provision, men are still more likely than women to have an uninterrupted work career, to be in full-time employment, and to be in the primary labour market with job security and work-related privileges. Take as an example the situation of my parents, who were both teachers working throughout their lives, apart from two periods of two years when I and my sister were born. My father's pension was £140 per month; my mother had nothing as a result of having worked part-time in the private sector. His job carried full sick-pay entitlement; hers did not, and so on. Economists noted and accepted the specialization of functions between the sexes, and it was thought more efficient to educate and train men to a higher standard because they would work continuously and could be paid the higher family wage to support their women and children (see, for example, Becker, 1974). As we move towards equal pay for men and women we leave no place for the family wage to compensate.

In addition to the entitlements to deferred earnings from employers in the form of sick-pay and pensions, the social security system also allows access to a share of society's resources. This system is composed of two parts; insurance and welfare. National Insurance benefits are based on contribution records, which are again work-related with the result that men tend to have better rewards. The welfare system is based on need and subject to means testing. It is based on the household, not the individual's, situation, but it offers support at the level of subsistence only.

With equal opportunities legislation and the vastly increased participation of women in the labour market, men and women starting out on their adult lives may appear to be equal, but the demon of economic imbalance lurks beneath the surface. The playing field for the two sexes has not been levelled.

Money and Partnering

What happens when a young man and woman meet and choose to spend the next part of their lives together? Do they choose to cohabit or to marry? And what are the financial implications of their choice?

When teaching bright young law students, I find their approach to cohabitation, which is close to their own experience, is to value the freedom associated with making their own rules about relationships, confident in the capacity of their loving relationships to survive and flourish without the need for the bourgeois trappings of marriage. Their increasing preference for cohabitation echoes that of the society of which they are a part (see Chapter 1). My approach always seems depressingly old and cynical. But the majority of cohabitations I see in research are those of older couples after a divorce or separation, and demonstrate some of the difficulties of living together.

So often it is not realized that forming a cohabiting partnership means forgoing some of the protection that the legal status of marriage affords to weaker parties, even when there are children from the union. In particular, there is no special protection of the cohabiting mother's right to a share in the family home, or even to continue to occupy it. Property outside marriage is entirely governed by property law, without any of the protection offered by family law to those in difficulty. A woman who separates from her partner after cohabitation has no right to a property settlement, to a survivor's pension or to protection on bankruptcy. She does, however, have access to the Child Support Agency, through which she can claim support from her partner for herself as mother of their child on the same basis as if she had been married.

So is marriage the better bet?

As the bride leaves the church or register office, in one important respect she is like the shiny new car being driven out of the showroom: her market value drops. True, she may have access to more resources if she has married 'well'. And there is now protection against her property immediately transferring to her husband on marriage, as used to happen not so long ago (see Chapter 2). She gains access to the survivor benefits accruing to her husband's pension, she acquires protection for her occupancy of the matrimonial home in the case of bankruptcy (at least, for a year), and she adds to those parts of his National Insurance benefits which include an allowance for dependants. But things are not as different as they might seem. In her own right there are likely to be significant opportunity costs.

For quite sensible reasons the new bride is likely either to have given up her job, or to have taken a new one which fits in with her husband's job (Mansfield and Collard, 1988). If she has a routine clerical or retailing job and goes on to have two children, she is likely to forego ten years wages – perhaps £145,000 (Joshi, 1987). Taking time out of employment, and perhaps returning to work on a part-time basis, she loses not only the wages but also the increments and promotion opportunities that would have accompanied continuous employment. In addition, she damages her own occupational pension rights by changing jobs and not working full time.

There is also a second stage of economic loss, not yet fully documented, which affects more women than men: the time lost from work as a result of caring for elderly or sick relatives. With an ageing population it is now the case that at any one time more women are off work caring for elderly relatives than for children. Time off work in later career stages is more expensive than earlier stages, so that the figure of £145,000 might need to be doubled to give a true indication of the costs involved. At this point in the life cycle the sexual division of labour is simply following the path laid down by biological imperatives earlier on; the second career interruption is taken on by the partner who experienced the first. But at this stage there is no biological imperative. In theory it would be possible for men to undertake the caring role at this point, but the disparity between their earnings and those of their wives is likely to be too great to make this a realistic alternative.

As well as having the potential to inflict economic damage on the weaker party, marriage also provides some protection under the law in recognition of the special relationship of trust between the parties. For example, there is an increasing number of women who have signed guarantees for their husbands' business loans using the family home as security for the debt. For the small businessman this may be the only security available. If a wife jeopardizes the security of her family to help the man she trusts and relies upon and is subsequently threatened with homelessness if he cannot repay the loan, what part should the law play? Are women to be regarded as capable, independent adults who require no legal safeguards? Or are they to be regarded as under the protection and control of their husbands and so in need of special protection from the law? Is it to be assumed that women, now separately taxed, have full access to the financial situations of their husbands and so can make informed decisions, or that they may not even know what their husbands earn and so are operating in the dark? The courts have wavered between sympathy for the lenders who keep credit available in hard times and a wish to protect women by requiring that they are shown to have been offered independent advice.

There are many pitfalls as women approach economic independence. In high-income households husbands and wives are likely to enjoy a very considerable degree of financial independence from each other. In low-income households it is likely to be the woman who manages and thereby controls the family budget; often the income will not be earned but consist of transfer payments in the form of state benefits which she is left to juggle with. But in middle-income households the ethic of independence and partnership is strong, and financial plans are made together. Partners will commonly have separate bank accounts, an arrangement that may work well until children are born. Then the wife who has been used to managing her own money may find she has an independent account with no income flowing into it; in needing to ask her husband for money she transforms the dynamics of the marital economy.

Our newly wed couple needs to be aware of these hard truths when embarking on marriage, particularly if they are prone to using the egalitarian language of partnership and sharing. Will they share everything – especially if he has earned most of it? Perhaps, while they are together. But what if they part? And what if, after divorce, either forms another partnership and has a second family? Talking about sharing could be dangerous and misleading; perhaps the prayer-book phrase 'endowing with worldly goods' is more realistic.

Divorce starkly illuminates the economics of marriage. In many cultures it is no great financial disaster. Where the divorced woman can return to her father's house (as in some African countries), where remarriage is easy (as, for example, in Japan) or where the community is willing to support lone parents (as in Scandinavian countries) there is support available for the potentially vulnerable. We in the UK have invested a great deal in marriage, but we have not developed a comfortable way of providing for the needs of the woman with children who divorces and does not remarry, especially if her husband does remarry and removes a considerable part of the available resources for his new family. The problem is not resolved by current proposals for divorce reform (Law Commission, 1993) which, if implemented, will effectively provide divorce on request by one party. We have moved a long way from the Catholic-Christian view of marriage as a sacrament which cannot be broken, and from the Protestant-Lutheran tradition which permitted divorce following adultery, whereby the guilty party was regarded as notionally or canonically dead. We may, however, be drawing closer to our Judaistic roots by preparing for divorce by note of dismissal, although differentiating ourselves by allowing women as well as men to exercise this option.

When the 1969 Divorce Reform Act was implemented in 1971, supposedly introducing 'no-fault' divorce, the British courts retained considerable discretion concerning the financial aspects of settlements. Other countries with codified systems of law tradition-ally had clearer rules about financial settlements after divorce. But the common law countries made no move towards, for example, the American situation in adopting rules aimed at dividing the property of a marriage equally between the parties. In California these rules were found to make the position of women worse, especially as they accompanied no-fault divorce and so removed potential bargaining chips from the economically weaker party. If a woman could withhold the right to divorce, she could bargain for a larger share of the property. If she had children, a 50–50 split meant that one person could take half the property while the other three or four family members were left with the other half. This was a very individualistic approach; we were more willing to think of an ongoing relationship between divorced parents.

Under the 1971 legislation the courts were in effect relieved of anything more than a rubber stamping role in cases of undefended divorce, and legal aid was withheld from these cases which were dealt with under a special procedure that no longer required the parties to attend the court. But in dealing with the financial matters (known as ancillary matters, despite their importance) the courts were asked to try and put the parties in the position they would have been in had the marriage not broken down. This strange notion, formulated by Lord Scarman, is derived from seeing marriage in legal terms, not as a religious sacrament but as a civil contract that can be rescinded – that is, made as if it never was. As will be apparent from the economics of marriage, this is simply not possible. The car has been driven out of the showroom. The woman's economic position has been damaged and she is at a disadvantage in comparison with her husband. If she has children not only is she unable to earn without spending the best part of her income on substitute child care, but also – because she is most likely to have the children living with her after divorce (only one in ten lone-parent families are headed by fathers) – she must bear most of the direct costs of caring for them, including food, clothing, larger accommodation, higher fuel bills and so on.

When the legislation was passed there was little discussion of the economic impact of children on adults. The policy debate of the early 1970s tended to replicate the old marital dispute, and to be concerned with the amount of income to be paid over to the former wife by the divorced husband. A general rule of thumb, echoing canon law, was that the husband should devote around one-third of his income to his former wife. But this famous 'one-third' rule never appeared in legislation. And it was still the case that the conduct of the parties could influence the financial decisions made by courts. While this was still possible under changes introduced to the law in 1984 (which reduced to one year the period before which a divorce petition could be heard), courts have not taken conduct into account when deciding on settlements. Maintenance orders were sometimes made to the wife, sometimes to the mother and children together, and sometimes to the children directly. The choice tended to depend on whether the woman was likely to remarry, in which case she would probably seek an order for the children. If she was older and the children were approaching independence she would be more likely to seek support for herself.

The 1971 legislation for the first time gave the courts power to override the law of property by giving part of the husband's property (usually the family home) to the wife by making a property order. Additionally, under the law of property, a wife has the right to register her occupation if not ownership of the family home. The existence of these powers, together with orders for what used to be called alimony (wife maintenance), led to a backlash from some men, as typified in the Campaign for Justice in Divorce. This organization particularly represented the interests of remarried men and their new wives. It led the campaign calling for a 'clean break' following divorce, arguing that to end a marriage and yet leave a continuing financial relationship was unfair and unacceptable. The campaign was skilfully orchestrated, castigating the 'alimony drones' who were depicted as living in luxury on their maintenance. (Similar tactics are now in use in campaigning against the Child Support Agency.) It culminated in the 1984 Matrimonial and Family Proceedings Act, the current legislation governing divorce, which reverses the presumption that there will be support to a former wife and makes it clear that a clean break in financial terms is desirable. Any spousal support, sometimes called transitional or rehabilitative maintenance, is intended to be short term and aimed at helping a former wife back into the labour market. However, the Act is very clear that a clean break is not to be considered when there are children of a marriage. This aspect has been overlooked in recent debates about the Child Support Agency.

It is now easier for a property agreement, sometimes one which involves the house being sold immediately and the proceeds being shared only when the last of the children becomes independent (a device known as a Mesher Order), to be made on divorce. Wife support is becoming rare, and child support falls under the jurisdiction of the Child Support Agency. Of course, a man leaving a marriage and making a generous settlement of the family home loses both his home and part of the capital investment he was building up. He may well not be able to replicate in a second marriage the standard of living he was able to enjoy in his first marriage. This is where the disappointment of second wives and their claims of being treated as second class citizens arises. But the man has left the marriage with his earning capacity intact. He is not economically disadvantaged in the same way as is a woman with dependent children. And the second wife has married a man with prior commitments knowing what she was taking on -- just as she might have married someone with a disability or a special talent. If fault is to be taken out of divorce it is not sensible to reintroduce it later by claiming a right to a clean break or fresh start because the breakdown of the marriage was the fault of the other party.

Underlying all that I have described so far is a central theme: the financial aspects of parenthood. Now it is time to address it directly.

Money, Parents and Children

If the financial strains of parenting are painful enough within marriage, they are even more visible after a marriage ends. This is clearly the aspect of marriage and marriage breakdown where sentiments converge but practice diverges. Under current divorce legislation courts are required to give primary (but not paramount) consideration to the interests of children when making decisions about financial settlements. This formulation begs the crucial question of *which* children – the children of the marriage that is ending, of a new partnership, or of another parent who might form a partnership with either of the formerly married parties? The law has yet to comment.

In the past we have, in practice in the UK, been very clear about which children came first. A man who repartnered was permitted by the social security system to support the family he was currently living with, while the state was expected to support the first family. Three out of four divorced or separated women with children living with them are currently dependent on income support, a means-tested benefit which provides income at subsistence level.

This support can be seen as being willingly offered by a community that accepts the realities of serial monogamy. Alternatively, it can be seen as a burden placed on the taxpayer by individuals who are failing to meet their responsibilities. The UK in the 1990s is adopting the latter view. It underlies the hasty setting up of the Child Support Agency as the means of implementing the aims of the 1991 Child Support Act. This Act marks a radical shift in policy towards lone-parent families. If a man has two families he is now expected to provide for the first before coping with the second. The state is no longer willing to take on the responsibilities of the parents when marriage ends, unless there is absolutely no alternative.

Previously, the courts had been able to make elegant orders, maximizing the resources available to both parties after divorce and taking account of their particular circumstances. Now the British system resembles models operating in the United States (in Wisconsin in particular) and in Australia. In both these common-law countries the business of child support is deemed to be too important to leave to the discretion of the courts and their inefficient enforcement machinery. Instead, calculations are made about the proportion of income spent on a child within intact families to arrive at the amount of income a parent not living with the child is legally liable to pay in support. In this country there is now a formula which calculates the amount of money the state would otherwise allocate to the lone-parent family if it was dependent on income support, and seeks to recover a proportion of this sum from the absent parent according to his (or her) means. The absent parent is given some protection for his personal needs, and he is not required to bring the level of income coming into his current household below subsistence level in order to support his former family.

First and subsequent families are now expected to live at the same kind of level. The calculations of the Child Support Agency are made on the basis of the blood tie between parent and child, irrespective of the marital status of the parents, and without any regard to any new partners and their resources. If the parent looking after the child, most often the mother, forms another partnership with a rich and generous man, this does not reduce the liability of the biological, non-resident father. If this father, in turn, takes on the responsibilities of a new partner and her children, his liability is not diminished until the income of the new household falls to income support levels. A revolution is occurring which both levels the resources of first and subsequent families and sweeps away the distinction between children of married and non-married parents. The financial liability debate has moved away from the old arguments about spousal maintenance towards a new focus on the responsibility of parents towards their children.

What are the implications for marriage of this shift in emphasis away from partnering and towards parenting responsibilities? I have summarized some of the financial inequalities that are built into marriage and the reasons for it. It is likely that they do not match well with the expectations of equality that women and men bring into marriage. Insofar as couples think about divorce there are also likely to be some surprises in store. Do the values of equality relate to what is put into a marriage or what is taken out of it? And do the same values apply to remarriage? I would suggest that the language of sharing and equality that is so prevalent in the discussion of marital expectations and aspirations conceals some hard economic realities, especially when partners become parents and ex-partners.

Mavis Maclean

9
A Woman's Place?

In Ken Loach's acclaimed film *Raining Stones* an unemployed Midlands working-class man is determined that his daughter shall have a new, not borrowed, outfit for her coming Confirmation. He senses the importance of this to his wife as well, even though she is only exploring the possibility and is far from insisting on it. Wounded by the poverty that constrains and impinges on the expression of his masculinity through an inability to provide economically, our hero secures a loan with a marginal lending firm in order to deliver the goods.

There is a moment of deep pleasure between husband and wife. He has been a man: he has delivered. His daughter is given the Confirmation outfit. But the heroism of the act unravels: the debt is sold to the loan sharks, who then act as loans sharks do. They rampage and destroy our hero's home and threaten the safety of his wife and daughter. The attempt to redeem self-esteem and worth by engaging in heroic behaviour based on old-fashioned macho values backfires. The price of pride is too high. But his wife, understanding what it means to him and why he felt he had to provide by whatever means, forgives him. The destruction he has unintentionally wrought is understood and excused.

Ken Loach's movie is told from the man's point of view. It romanticizes, extols and valourizes the struggle of a middle-aged, unemployed man to keep his dignity and come through for his wife and daughter by engaging single-handedly in risky acts that cause great destruction. Nowhere in the movie do we see the husband and wife talk with one another about the dilemma they face over their daughter. Does she or doesn't she need a new dress? If yes, how should they go about it? What does it mean to him that he and his mates are excluded from participating in the consumerist society that surrounds them? How does he feel about scrabbling around for work that pays tuppence ha'penny? How do they survive as a family and couple when their dreams of life are shattered by the economic reality of the mass unemployment they have little say about?

Ken Loach doesn't invite these questions; instead he creates emotional pressure for us to empathize with a man's choice to fight back alone, to refuse to be a victim. The movie is billed as a comedy about survival, but in disregarding the woman and child's point of view, the comedy relies on our applauding macho values rather than interrogating them to provide a different version of how a man can act.

I start with this anecdote because it is an everyday example of the gendered ways in which we approach the difficulties that can occur in marriage. Ken Loach, one of our most progressive filmmakers, whose finger has been on the social pulse since *Cathy Come Home*, *Wednesday's Child*, *Kes* and *Riff Raff*, loses his critical eye when he turns to gender, marriage and relationships. He ends up commending rather than reflecting on the way in which this man – whose masculinity and sense of self is jeopardized by the economic mess of our time – refuses, in the most macho and self-defeating of ways, to accept victimhood. The film was enjoyed by many critics, and won awards at Cannes and Berlin. Their applause and honour suggest some of the reasons why there is such a very deep rift between women and men at this moment in history. When in a corner men are inclined to act, specifically, and often in a circumspect manner. The dramatic appeal of this is at odds with the attainment of intimacy – one of the crucial factors people seek in marriage-type relationships.

The Smallest Mental Hospital

The eminent psychoanalyst Harold Searles's profound description of marriage as 'the smallest mental hospital' (1955) is an observation I could readily apply to the confusions, hurt, misery and disappointment that marks so much of contemporary marriage as seen by a psychotherapist.

The madnesses played out in marriage have much to do with the unconscious contracts between women and men when they come together in an intimate relationship. These contracts are concerned with unconscious expectations, with what has been observed of the parental marriage and the marriages of significant others, with the kind of intimacy experienced in the first love relationship with mother, and with what is projected unknowingly on to a partner (Eichenbaum and Orbach, 1982, 1983; Clulow and Mattinson, 1989; Ruszczynski, 1993; Young-Eisendrath, 1993).

We bring to marriage a desire to express and receive love, to exchange companionship, erotic intimacy, our needs for attachment, and to fulfil a wish to have our individuality supported and extended from the base of a stable and secure relationship. Almost everything we desire from marriage, including the hearts-and-flowers imagery which pervades our notions of romance, express in their deepest

conceptions differences between men and women in their understanding of these desires.

In love and in marriage we start from the premise that men and
women are speaking the same emotional language. We assume that
closeness and intimacy, sharing and caring, selfhood, individuality
and coupledom relate to the same ideas. We assume that our
imaginative worlds include reference points that cross gender. To a
considerable extent this is true – but it is not always so. While we
recognize that profoundly different skills and roles are employed by
a father or a mother in parenting – as well as overlapping ones – while
we even value and valourize those differences, we are hazy about the
very profound significance of gender-honed differences and dis-
similarities when we come to the nitty-gritty of intimacy.

This haziness – the denial of our conscious and unconscious
gendered desires, our confusion about the sexual politics of the
contract between women and men – lead, in part, to the distress that
Searles refers to when he speaks of marriage as the smallest mental
hospital. We go 'mad' in marriage because our expectations and
hopes conflict deeply with our experience. We imagine, dream of and
anticipate a relationship with one set of parameters; we discover that
we are enmeshed in one whose parameters are foreign. We become
dislocated, anguished, confused and often shamed. In that frame of
mind we act from fear and from the most defensive and reactive
aspects of our selves. We are then at our least creative. When we are
disillusioned in love we are hurt – and when we are hurt, we want to
inflict hurt.

I wish to look at women's place in marriage, and her perception of
her place (and, briefly, a woman's perception of a man's view of his
place) from a perspective that recognizes the differences between
women and men, and sees gender and the psychic and social
construction of feminity and masculinity as both descriptive and
critical categories.

In describing what occurs from a woman's perspective in many
intimate relationships, I also wish to suggest that there is a need for
serious revisions in the contract of intimacy. Indeed, the search for
intimacy as it is presently conducted by women within heterosexual
relations often flounders not because 'men are bastards', but because
the skills and expectations women bring to marriage clash with those
brought by men.

Central to the painful, divisive differences that contribute to the
breakdown of the contemporary couple is a destructive set of

culturally defined meanings that surround the concept of dependency. In Loach's film, the man's need to meet the economic needs of his family, and to perceive them as economically dependent upon him, leads to a situation in which he endangers himself, his wife, his child and all that is most dear to him. The compulsion to act on the economic front, ennobled in the film, is a contract we all understand. In the old script, the man 'brought home the bacon', while in exchange the woman supplied caregiving, housekeeping and emotional services. She depended on him for money, he depended on her to iron his shirts, cook the dinner and take care of his aunties' birthday. Behind this contract – a contract that has been in disarray for the last two decades but, as Loach's film shows, can still unquestioningly entice and ensnare us – is concealed a more problematic contract: the disposition of emotional dependency needs between women and men (Eichenbaum and Orbach, 1983).

The Disposition of Dependency

'Dependency' is a dirty word and a disparaged idea in our culture. Right-wing ideologues, anxious to dismantle the welfare state, have scorned our state services as the illness of a dependency culture that weakens and enervates its members. The attack has been persuasive not because of its inherent correctness, but because dependency touches a sensitive nerve in all of us; we may not be sure why, but we wish to disassociate ourselves or flee from it. Dependency is somehow weak, connected with notions of subservience, linked in the thesaurus with 'possession' and 'loss of agency', and therefore something to be abhorred.

The emotional appeal that politicians can rely upon in condemning dependency resonates psychologically with the idea that dependency is to be avoided. But why do we consider dependency so awful? Why must we avoid, despise and condemn it?

Psychoanalytic therapists are impelled in their work, which is always a work of both research and care, to explore the unconscious meanings of problematic issues, rather than simply to accept and collude with conscious and manifest meanings. The psychoanalytic researcher wonders why dependency is so feared and dreaded, and why a call to deny or defeat dependency can be so invigorating. What is it in the developmental schema that makes dependency so troublesome?

The mother-infant relationship is marked by the dependency of the infant on the mother. This dependency is so profound that

Winnicott (1965), the distinguished paediatrician and psychoanalyst, pointed out that in order for a mother to properly understand and interpret the needs of her utterly dependent baby, she must fall psychologically 'ill' herself – into a state that will allow her to identify with and feel attuned to the baby's experience of need. Out of her understanding of and identification with that experience she will understand what she needs to give. And out of her own experience of being responded to in that emotional state, she will find the wherewithal to provide.

If all goes well, the baby will take in the emotional nurture provided. It will feel comfortable relying on mother's external presence, her breast, her smell, her holding, her voice and contact, as it once did in the womb. The food for the baby's emotional and physical growth will come from the mother. Her ability to interpret its needs will be 'ingested' by the baby and form the core of its sense of self and separate subjectivity.

As mother moves from being an umbilical cord or breast to a real person in the baby's world, the baby will, from a safe and secure base, explore other relationships. It will develop its own motor, cognitive and language skills, and move on from the state of utter helplessness to one in which it can make relationships with others. It will move from dependence to interdependence, recognizing its need for others as well as its separateness from them. It will come out of babyhood into childhood and adolescence, and eventually into adulthood. It will develop a sense that intimacy and love are to be welcomed and savoured.

Dependency in this schema is linked with infancy. It is in theory an unproblematic aspect of a phase of development that results in adults who are able, ready and willing to make relationships with others similarly disposed towards interdependence. But infant dependency is rarely so straightforward.

Dependency is entwined for nearly all of us with notions of helplessness. The infant who is unable to ensure that his or her initiatives are recognized, or needs are met, finds the state of dependency less than the warm, containing, emotional cradle of Winnicott's idealized mother-baby pair gliding towards mutual recognition and interdependence, and more a state of potential disappointment, fear and treachery. Frustrated by and unable to comprehend the actions of a caretaker on whom he or she had depended, the idea is born that to depend is to place oneself in jeopardy. Herein lies the dilemma: although there is a wish to depend no longer on a felt-to-be unreliable caregiver, the dependency needs remain. Neither having embodied sufficient emotional sustenance to bid farewell to the intensity of need, nor trusting another to respond to such needs, a person is caught.

This dependency dilemma, and the associated dilemma of help-lessness, has the potential to affect us all as adult human beings. Good-enough parenting prevents the more extreme instances of helplessness: it can provide the child with an emotional ambience that enables experiences of ordinary helplessness to be metabolized. That is to say, the child, later the adult, can recognize its needs, can recognize when he or she is feeling helpless, and can acknowledge the pain of those feelings; the person can live through and beyond them. He or she can tolerate the distress which helplessness causes without having to conceal it and without being overwhelmed by its expression. Having experienced and survived the feelings with another, they become transformed, and a sense of equilibrium is restored.

But for many, the prophylactic is insufficient. In place of a capacity to process dependency needs and feelings of helplessness, there is a dysfunctional response – away from engaging with the difficult feelings, and towards expending energy to defend against such feelings.

The Gender Contract

In the human struggle to come to terms with unmet dependency needs, men and women are offered and find gendered solutions. They find themselves as individuals in the dilemma of wanting to be attached and connected, both because adults need to be connected to others generally, and because they need the love and attention of a specific intimate relationship to bring their dependency needs to. The problems that stalled aspects of personal development may then find new pathways to resolution. But they simultaneously fear a close relationship that will reactivate buried hurts from the past, expose them to what is now a dreaded state of dependency, and evoke unsatisfactory patterns of relating in the present.

The gendered solutions set in train in early childhood and fashioned through adulthood evolve into entrenched patterns that are so much a part of who one is, and so central to self-experience, that they cannot be shifted without unhinging identity. The individual does not feel them as constraints of gender; he or she does not feel they are acting 'feminine' or 'masculine'; they feel themselves to be acting in ways that are personal and idiosyncratic, which, of course, they are. But as I think will become clear, these personal ways are guided by subtle, and not so subtle, gender influences.

Girls are encouraged to deal with unmet dependency needs by providing for others. Starting at an early age they are guided to be solicitous, thoughtful and caring of others, just like their mothers. They practise the skills of emotional relatedness, of sorting out one another's problems, and they develop a facility for interpreting the emotional temperature of others. When hurt they are briefly consoled, but then taught to turn their attention to the needs of others, to bigger hurts that need addressing, or to be self-sacrificing in order not to inflict pain or distress on others. In their passage through adulthood, they come to be sensitive to the effects of their actions on others, and pay considerable attention to their needs by being helpful. They are practising what will later become a crucial aspect of identity: how to be alert, to tune their radar to pick up the emotional needs and desires of others.

Thus the girls, and later the women, are transposing their own needs for emotional attention into the capacity to meet those needs in others (Orbach, 1978; Eichenbaum and Orbach, 1982). They are giving to others what they long for themselves. They know about deprivation, they know about longing for recognition and for their needs to be taken into account. Out of that knowledge, which Winnicott declared women needed in order to mother, they will identify with the needs of the person whose shoes they step into when they give to them. When they give, they are attempting to assuage their own needs; when they give, they are seeking a kind of gratification; when they give, they are soothing themselves with their apparent needlessness. They can give because they know what's needed. They will provide emotional services without the other even being aware of them, or even being aware of the need in the first place.

The boy, in the meantime, is learning and practising a different set of emotional responses to his neediness. As he learns to be separate from his mother, he distances himself from the early intimacy by taking on a stance of being not like mother. While he may not have the model of a father to identify with on a consistently available basis – fathers spend considerably less time with their children than mothers – he will learn a different code and set of solutions to the problems of his unmet dependency needs. He will be offered the solution of appearing not to need, of denying his own needs, not through taking care of others and melding in with their needs as a girl might do, but by detaching himself from others and appearing need-free. He will bolster this self-image through competing and defining his separateness. His self-identity involves making a space between himself and others.

By the time the boy reaches adulthood, a range of heroic man-on-his-own imagery will be available for him to identify with: if it is no longer the Marlboro Man, or the cowboy, or James Bond, then it is the axiomatic hero of the modern movie – Ken Loach's protagonist, Coppola's tragic heroes, Kevin Costner's politically correct saviour, or Mel Gibson's Mad Max. Their most passionate feelings are for conquering, defeating, performing heroics or leading – not for sharing or exposing vulnerability .

The point of these men is that they don't need, and rarely depend on, anyone. In fact, by a curious sleight of hand, their wives and girlfriends are deemed to need them. Not only can they deny their dependency needs, but also, like the women, they too can feel they are there to serve the needs of others.

In the last 100 years, men have demonstrated this giving role through being the strong and financially providing one. Their silence is interpreted as knowing and wise rather than an unknowing paralysis that for many men it really is. With the collapse of the economic arrangement between women and men the veil of dependency has been lifted, exposing the emotional nurturance transactions concealed behind it. Men and women are in crisis because the old bargain – in which she provided emotional and household services and he provided economic stability – has broken down. Ken Loach's 1990s man tries to resurrect that arrangement: he wants the money and the dress both to express and symbolize his love and attention.

Recently, I worked with a couple where the wife complained about being neglected by her husband, and he complained about her constant misery and inability to find something interesting to do. She was a transported wife, having given up her career in the United States to follow him to England so they could continue to live together as a family when his work brought him over. He worked at least 12 to 14 hours a day, five or six days a week. She was lonely and felt abandoned, and although she could easily pin her distressed feelings on his actual absence from home, she knew that to be too convenient a peg. There was something deeper going on that all her histrionic complaining could not move him to consider.

Her husband was a senior banker. Two-hundred people reported to him. He couldn't go to the toilet without being followed by colleagues, so much was his attention valued. He felt beleaguered by his wife, who seemed to want so much from him; he gave her money, a nice home, good holidays – what more could she want?

He felt a deep sense of inadequacy when it came to relating to the emotional needs of his wife, which was experienced as demands that he dealt with by designating her as over-needy and hysterical: nothing was ever enough for her. True, she did a lot for him, and she had smoothed his domestic and social path in England by settling the children, sorting out a butcher and doctor, assembling a group of friends, and so on. But, he remonstrated, he was there when he could be – *and* he had just bought her a new diamond.

In therapy the wife took on board the idea that she was expecting her husband to meet emotional needs she could not articulate for herself, needs which had arisen since they had been together and which were to be given attention and to be made to feel 'all better'. These needs engendered shame in her. She recognized that she brought some of them to the relationship from her childhood; that her disappointment with her mother had made her look to men to fill the hole inside her. Through playing house, looking after her children and husband and, more lately, through working, she had covered much of the void. As she began to address this void, she reduced the attention claimed from her husband, and was no longer clingy and demanding.

On a business trip which took her husband away from home for seven days, she got on with her own thing and, unusually, was even away from the telephone during a couple of the times he tried to reach her. When he returned to London he was in a bad state, and unconsciously provoked her insecurity by insinuating that one of his female colleagues had flirted with him on the trip and that he had been tempted. He was upset by the instability he felt in being out of touch with his wife, and unsettled by what he saw as her withdrawal. Although he disliked the way she would invade his space, or velcro herself to him, even less did he like the boomeranging of his own needs back on himself. The void caused by her withdrawal unconsciously led him to try to pull her back into a pattern which, while it annoyed him, also reassured him that he was not the needy one. She needed him and he could be irritated by that; that was a much less terrifying option than recognizing his dependency on or need of her. It emerged that he was also deeply dependent on other people needing him at work. Although he resented her demanding behaviour, it soon became apparent that when it was no longer displayed, he was emotionally adrift and at sea.

Their marriage was, as Searles said, a mental hospital. The seesaw in which her needs concealed his needs was finely balanced. One kind of madness was when the balance was upset; another kind of madness followed the attempt to restore it. If the mental hospital was to offer a cure, it would have to provide the conditions in which they could each recognize and reclaim their own needs and insecurities, show them to one another, have them recognized, and then strive to address them through the acknowledgement of their mutual inter-dependence.

Demons, Dependency and the Missing Dialogue

In the 1994 Reith Lectures, Marina Warner spoke of the contempo-rary myths of rapacious women and marauding men that reflect our understanding of what it means to be men and women today. The evidence she drew on owed much to history re-told from a feminist perspective. Drawing on many disciplines, she showed how gender constructs our desires and sense of ourselves, and how we position ourselves in relation to the other sex. Boys, obsessed with computer games which search, kill and destroy, contrast heavily with girls who acquire relational skills and then seek to express them in an intimate relationship. But in our collective psyche, the mythological character of the warrior, which is assigned to men and which young boys emulate, is now embattled with the powerful female who must be controlled. As women's demand has grown for the authorship of their actions, so the demonization of women has increased. As Warner argues, it is no accident that the Jurassic Park's Raptor Dinosaurs are female – the feminization of the ultimate marauders.

The demonization of women at a cultural level is not strictly a conscious act. Indeed, we might argue that far from demonizing women we idealize them. We protect this idealization by splitting them into categories of good and bad – madonna/whore; good mother/single mother – we separate out their troublesomeness and relate to their goodness. But when couple therapists confront marriages in difficulty, what becomes immediately obvious is that the saintly qualities projected on to women have become tainted – men and women can no longer hold on to the culturally created fiction of women that have been created.

Gender constructs our relationship to intimacy, and to a crucial aspect of intimacy, namely dependency. What Loach's film demon-strates is the vast difference between men and women's conceptions of intimacy. Men, stripped of the capacity to provide in the ways masculinity demands, do what they can to extend state provisions and make their wives and daughters happy by supplying what they think is wanted of them. Women provide emotional labour for families and relationships, accepting the anguish of men, supporting and forgiving them, even when they are a danger. Nowhere in the film, and sometimes in real life, are other alternatives explored – ones which depend on communicating, talking, facing disappointment together, taking emotional responsibility and exploring feelings of distress as an adult.

Marriage and intimate relationships touch us deeply. Through the particular nature of the bond that is created, childhood yearnings, as well as adult longings for care, nurture and attachment are stimulated in particular ways. The adaptations that allow us to survive in work relationships or in friendships unravel in the merged nature of intimacy. This unravelling makes us crazy, partly because of our early histories and partly because the nature of the gendered exchange is incomprehensible from our different perspectives. We find ourselves in a 'mental hospital' which becomes a place of madness and a place of retreat. But if the gender and dependency dynamics can be recognized and addressed, we have a way out – we have a way of using the 'mental hospital' as a place of healing so that the magical and wonderful aspects of intimacy which rest on mutual dependency and respect can remedy the misunderstandings and disappointments that dog so many marriages today.

Susie Orbach

10
A Man's Place?

If a woman's place is in the home, then a man's place is out of it. This is not the sort of thing one says nowadays, but in most societies, in most periods of history, it has been the accepted view of the matter. So why not stop there?

This book is about predicaments in contemporary marriage. It is not possible to say that marriage has been a great success in the past, but it is clearer now than ever before that the institution is severely strained. One agreed fact is that the majority of divorces are started by wives, suggesting that they see before their husbands do that there is no point in going on. So what is wrong with so many men that they cannot see what is happening in their relationships? My provisional reply to that question is that men have typically been in difficulties with relationships for a very long time, thousands of years in fact, and that it is about time we revised our ideas about what men are for.

Most of the concepts, even obligations, of manhood that come to mind without much reflection are to do with fighting, sexuality and fathering; the three 'f's' if you like. First of all, a man has to be brave, strong and heroic. He should not complain if he is in pain or afraid. He should win the struggle, whatever it is, and when he finally gets home he should bring with him the dead body of whatever it was he was in contest with, whether enemy or prey. This is the fighting, hunting male, and he is derived from the image of a wild, hairy beast that is bigger and stronger than all the others, like a great ape. Of course, he will have been afraid during his exploits, but somehow this is not to be discussed.

Then there is another side of his character which is his virility. This is to do with his sexual potency. We need to distinguish his actual ability from what he says about it. The vital importance of potency runs throughout the history of manhood, and failure is not to be considered. His actual activity in sexual intercourse may in fact be totally different from his talk. In reality he may be tender and affectionate as well as thrusting and powerful. A man's relationship with a woman begins more or less the same way as a woman's in infancy, and however big and strong he is, there is still the baby boy inside that wants to cuddle up to mummy.

The third aspect of his character is the father, traditionally stern and unyielding, remote and terrifying. Even some modern men confess that before their own children were born they believed that their primary task was to punish them. But the man's actual life with his children may be quite different, if he allows it, so that he can be gentle and attentive with them, as well as fierce and firm, just like a mother is.

All of these facets of the man's character are performances. Now, the performing male has a problem, in my view. He used to be able to get away with it, but the need for this particular show is fading fast.

Until the Second World War, men could reasonably be seen as soldiers in reserve. Images of men from that time could only be cast in this upright mode. But since then there has been a change which will never be reversed. The smokestack-phase of the Industrial Revolution is over. Men's work in factories, and, most powerfully, down the mine, is more or less finished. Most jobs are now dependent on technology of some kind. Muscle power, which is virtually the only physical advantage of the male, is no longer necessary, except for furniture removal and a few other tasks that defiantly resist electronic wizardry.

With these very few exceptions, women can do anything that men can do. The fact that they don't is no longer a physical but a political phenomenon. The best-paid and most prestigious jobs are still held by men. I am not sure that these jobs are in reality so desirable. Who really wants to spend half the night in the House of Commons, or in a faraway hotel room negotiating a big deal? The answer is, of course, that many men, and some women, do want this because it seems to be exciting. There is no denying the anti-depressant effect of work in institutions: even quite humdrum activities can give you the feeling that you are helping some giant wheel to turn.

It is odd that the most important job of all, looking after children, has such low status. This has something to do with the assumption that it is only women's work. I think we also have to recognize that, apart from the special moments of wonder that parents can have with children, a lot of childcare is a chore. You can enjoy children without spending hours in their company. Children see it differently: they would like to spend hours in your company, even if you do not have to attend to them directly. Parents – and it usually is mothers – are expected to be if not actually in the room, somewhere nearby. Now that women have found freedom in paid work, they are prepared to pay someone else to look after the children. The prime privilege of the father – working outside the home – has been badly dented. Of course, the average pay of men is higher than for women, and women still finish up doing low-status jobs that few men would touch, but all that is gradually changing.

So the clear definition of the man's place is losing its sharpness. Most of the women who have taken advantage of these changes would not think for a moment that this had anything to do with feminism, yet it must have played its part.

It is because the woman's place has changed that the man's has to do so. He did not initiate the change, although he could welcome it if he understood it. It is women who have fought to be educated, to understand the outside world, to use their wisdom and intelligence to make things different. Mostly, men resisted this because it undermined their fragile hold on the world. It may seem odd to describe male prestige as fragile, but this is just the point: if you are not sure of yourself, you have to make yourself more important than you are. Women's advance over the past few hundred years has accelerated in recent decades, but I am more concerned here to discuss the advance of men that preceded it long ago.

The Rise of Patriarchy in Neolithic Times

Up to about 10,000 years ago, men and women lived relatively simple lives in the open, sometimes in caves. Yet they had developed sophisticated social and ritual activities that gave meaning to life. They buried their dead, and had done so for tens of thousand of years; they could light fires and paint brilliant pictures on cave walls. What they could not do was to grow plants and harvest them. We may think this a distinct disadvantage, but the gathering and hunting lifestyle can be quite an easy one. After all, the food is there to be had; you do not have to work for it. This is how other animals live.

It is usually assumed, or was until recently, that early humans depended on meat to live and, because they were the hunters, on men to survive. Modern scholars and anthropologists have other ideas (Tanner, 1981).

Most of the food eaten by people in pre-agricultural societies is gathered by hand. It need not be vegetable. It is quite possible to get good-quality protein from small animals and insects, even if we might not be keen to eat them ourselves. You have to remember that the world was not very crowded in prehistoric times. Also much of it was covered with ice, and people tended to live in warmer parts such as Africa and the Middle East (even modern hunter-gatherers such as the ! Kung say that life is easy, and wonder why other people struggle so hard to grow food when you can just pick it). Interestingly, the skeletal remains of early people show that the first farmers had, on average, smaller bodies than the hunter-gatherers that preceded them, suggesting that the quality of the new diet was actually poorer (Diamond, 1991). We think of bread or rice as staple human foods, but before 10,000 years ago such grains would only be an incidental part of the diet. Life was not necessarily nasty and brutish, although it was shorter than now.

Here is an account of how it might have been in those days (Ehrenberg, 1989):

> Everyone has sufficient food and there is little stress and jealousy as everyone has equal access to the very few commodities available . . . if women were, on the whole, responsible for gathering plant foods and perhaps small animals, this may not have taken many hours a day. Unlike hunting, which depends on quietness, plant gathering could be quite a social activity, carried out by all the able-bodied women of a band working together. Young children could play round about, receiving attention whenever necessary, or remain at the homebase with elderly relatives. (p.62)

This is a picture of stable domestic life. Note the similarity with the modern family, whether nuclear or not. The father is absent, at work. The difference is, however, that his work was not absolutely necessary. He would return with a dead animal from time to time, maybe a gigantic one like a mammoth, which could indeed feed the band for weeks, but these were bonuses rather than essentials. No doubt it is good to have a roast for Sunday dinner, but if you have a reasonable diet during the week, that will do well enough.

I think the idealization of the hunting male was an invention. He is very skilful and brave, it is true, but he is not the breadwinner (notice how the term 'breadwinner' relates to the post-agricultural world in which wealth was measured in wheat, not meat). Furthermore, he is not the patriarch either. The misty picture of the prehistoric family (you can imagine the Victorians portraying this very well) is a large, bearded man holding a dead beast, standing over his wife and children, master of all he surveys. My understanding of this impressive archetype is that it was developed later, out of our – that is men's – wish to be just as important as women. In prehistoric life, it is much more likely that the man and the woman were more equal, and that the man played his part without any sense of superiority. He was probably less well-equipped with detailed knowledge of plants and small animals than her, and less involved in the care of the children. His bonds with other males, as in other primate species, may have been quite strong, as they would face death together on hunting trips. At best he could be a helpful consort to the mother of his children.

If either sex felt superior, it was likely to be the women (Lerner,

1986). After all, they had the greatest gift, which was the capacity to produce babies. This was a mysterious process, and it is possible that the 'facts of life' as we quaintly call them, were not known, or at least not given much significance, until the Agricultural Revolution. It is clear that life could go on without these facts, although once they were known, of course things had to change. There is a curious paradox here: before men knew about their part in making babies they were relatively modest; after discovering what a tiny part it was, they became inflated: 'The discovery of physiological paternity is the discovery at the same time of men's inclusion in and exclusion from natural reproductive process.' (O'Brien, 1981)

Following the Agricultural Revolution that began in the Middle East about 10,000 years ago, the status of males changed dramatically. In evolutionary terms, what happened was quite rapid. After millennia of gathering and hunting, the idea that seeds could be planted and grown took over within a few hundred years. It started in the Fertile Crescent of the Levant, where conditions were just right for the growth of wheat-like grasses. Farming began on a small scale, so that women and men could share tasks equally, using a hoe to turn the soil, and learning about the sexual lives of animals as they became domesticated. This is probably when the penny dropped: they discovered that humans are mammals too, and have the same organs as cows and pigs, although in slightly different places. The domestication of plants and animals included the domestication of humans.

But, being ingenious, these early agriculturalists soon saw that they could make bigger farms. This is where the male's superior strength came into its own. The first ploughs were made around 4,000 BC, and their invention made it possible to cultivate far larger areas than before. This work would have been done by men, putting them in a position to take charge of the surpluses they made. As soon as you move from subsistence to surplus, you are in the business of business (Engels, 1884). And the same goes for animal herds: a large herd needs tending by shepherds and cowboys, as we might now call them, who would spend much of their time away from the home base. For women, this was not possible as long as they had dependent children to look after. They also had a lot of extra work to do, making food and other items from animal products: milk, skins and so on. The management of big herds and the discovery that you could train an animal to pull a plough, and later to pull a wheeled cart, led to the first experiments in genetic engineering – namely, the castration of weaker males and the promotion of the stud. Here was a very good model for the increasingly powerful man to follow. Furthermore, ploughs were at first made of wood but later of metal, the fashioning of which has remained one of the preserves of men for most of history. The maker of iron tools could also make weapons.

The Demise of the Goddesses

Not surprisingly, similar changes were going on in the mythical world of the deities. In the old days, the principal objects of worship were female, or just animals and spirits, like the wind. But the decline of the goddesses seems to have been fairly continuous from the start of the Agricultural Revolution. At the beginning of history, the cities of Sumer, in Mesopotamia, flourished between 4,000 and 3,000 BC. There, the first written records were made. Judging from the stories left behind, the male and female gods and goddesses were moving in opposite directions, one in the ascendant and the other declining. Inanna, the Queen of Heaven, the goddess of love and war, was worshipped there, but the stories about her reveal that she was struggling to maintain superiority over a competitive husband as well as a jealous sister (Sanday, 1981). Male gods were appearing, apparently with the intention of taking over (Fisher, 1979). Later, Inanna becomes Anath of Canaan. After that she disappears as a goddess, only to reappear, according to several authors (Sanday, 1981; Baring and Cashford, 1991) as Eve in the Garden of Eden, and then later as the Virgin Mary. In the Mediterranean, around Greece, there was a similar story. Preceding the legends of classical Greece, the chief deity of the Aegeans was the Great Goddess, the Universal Mother (Johnson, 1988; Neumann, 1955), who was sometimes called Rhea (Guirand, 1959). But she is later upstaged by her son Zeus, after which she significantly becomes just one of his many wives. Zeus was the god of the sky, and the most powerful god who saw everything and knew everything, not unlike the God of the Bible and the Qur'an.

In other parts of the world there arose a whole host of father-creators. In ancient China the August Personage of Jade prevailed: 'He was the first god . . . [who] created human beings . . . by modelling them in clay. He is referred to as Father-Heaven' (Guirand, 1959, p.381). And from India came 'Brahma . . . the first person of the Hindu Trinity . . . the father of gods and of men.' He unfolds the universe and 'by thought produced the waters and deposited his seed in them. This seed became a golden egg as brilliant as the sun . . . In this egg the blessed one remained a whole year, then of himself, by the effort of his thought only, he divided the egg into two. From the two halves he made heaven and earth . . .' (Guirand,

1959, p.344). This god is unusual in that he is regarded as being fallible and is said to have made a number of mistakes, so the process of creation proceeded by advances and setbacks. He is depicted with four heads (Senior, 1985).

Much later in history, the Slavs had a sun and fire god Svarog, who was the father of all the other gods. In Teutonic mythology, the giant Ymir, the first of all living beings, was formed from the thawing of the ice (Guirand, 1959), and gave birth to the first male-and-female couple from his sweaty armpit (Walker, 1983). Lacking a vagina, many gods gave birth from their mouths. Other methods included a lethal form of Caesarian section, hatching from a male-incubated egg, or birth through the penis. Zeus also managed to defy anatomy. Having swallowed his wife Metis, he gave birth to Athene from his head. These are different portrayals of ingenious, mythical fathers, all of whom created humans without female help.

These remarkable feats of biological acrobatics were required to prop up the new man of the day, very different to the one of the same name we are busy trying to find. The fact is that within the space of about a thousand years man had, decisively and impressively, created god in his own image. With agricultural surpluses to distribute in return for favours and loyalty, the charismatic 'big men' could also take political leadership (Service, 1975). These were the prototype kings and emperors, who saw themselves as fathers of all their people.

How did father-creators come to occupy such a prominent place in so many religions? If you did not know how infants were conceived, you would not worship a man because he does not have babies – he does not make people. You would say that, in the beginning, the first human came out of a female, which is, of course, the truth. Yet by the time and in the places that these myths were established, the truth had been abandoned. It looks as though when man realized the facts of life he could not face them, so he changed them. Here is a passage from the *Oresteia* trilogy by Aeschylus: 'The mother is not the parent of the child/Which is called hers. She is the nurse who tends the growth/Of young seed planted by its true parent, the male.' (cited by Lerner, 1986, p.205)

It is quite likely that women would have supported men in the technological and economic advancement of agriculture because it seemed a good idea to build bigger and better businesses. If you assume there was no battle of the sexes before that time (some sort of Garden of Eden) then why would there be any reason to stop them? What we now regard as 'natural' differences between men and women were being created in most unnatural ways, that is, by culture.

Rivalry and Envy

The fact that male deities replaced female ones, and took over their reproductive powers, strongly suggests an envious attack on women (Kraemer, 1991). Relative equality gave way to the inequality of the sexes of the historic world. Men's status, or prestige, was increased, but at great cost to their modesty, their capacity to love, and, of course, to women. As feminist scholars have shown, the political, intellectual and artistic achievements of women throughout history have been largely ignored. But because vulnerability and tenderness are projected into women, the definition of maleness becomes rather hollow, encouraging performance at the expense of genuineness:

> It is as if the symbol of authority is a hard father who is not yet assured of loving and being loved, a narcissistically wounded or deprived person who, despairing of being loved, resorts to force and legalistic principles and reinforces this way of feeling secure by accentuating masculine-feminine polarities and subjugating females and female deities. (Redfearn, 1992, p.188)

Something happened to men all those years ago that is only now becoming clear. This is partly because the story of the world was written by men who could not question their superior role in it. The fact is that men are just as necessary as women for keeping the species going, but that they do not have to be in charge. Until the smoke of the Industrial Revolution began to clear, we could not see this. It has been the task of many women scholars and writers to open our eyes to a different version of the story, and a different role for us. There is always a very fierce reaction to this sort of talk, and not only from men. The attempt to rebalance genders seems to disturb the very foundations of our thinking. This is so because notions of sex and gender *are* the foundation of much of our thinking, about roles, power, love, sexuality, social order; the very stuff of life and its meaning. Freud shocked the world with his observations that sexuality is part of everyone's life, even infants. Feminists, who have rarely been friends with Freud, have noted that our unconscious reliance on assumptions of gender is equally pervasive.

Men in Non-Western Societies

So far, I have been telling a story, rather a 'Just So' story, of how the man laid claim to his power over the woman: in his anxiety to assert his equal importance, he was overcome with a bitter envy that made him hate the woman he had previously admired. While thinking about this, it is instructive to look at other societies besides our own. We can readily imagine the privilege of the male in a Western setting, how he can talk louder and interrupt the female, how he can stare at her while her eyes are averted downwards. Even today this sort of process goes on all the time. The difference is that we can now talk about it and question if that is how things should be. In Japan, men and women use different parts of speech when saying precisely the same thing. So, as she proposes to leave the house, for example, a woman will say the same words but with different endings. The effect is that the female utterance is soft and sweet, while the male is tough and active.

In every society men are distinguished from women, in some quite violently. Here is a description of the boy's upbringing in the Yanomami people of Venezuela (Harris, 1993):

Yanomami boys learn cruelty by practising on animals. Lizot watched several male juveniles gathered round a wounded monkey. They poked their fingers into the wounds and pushed sharp sticks into its eyes. As the monkey dies, little by little, 'its every contortion stimulates them and makes them laugh' . . . The Yanomami's preferred form of armed engagement is the surprise raid at dawn. Under cover of darkness the members of the raiding party pick a trail outside the enemy village and wait for the first man or woman to come along at daybreak. They kill as many men as they can, take the women as captives, and try to leave the scene before the whole village can be roused . . . husbands beat their wives for disobedience, but especially for adultery . . . others beat their wives with clubs, swung at them with machetes and axes, or burned them with firebrands. Some shot barbed arrows into their wives' legs. (pp.64–5)

Yet the Yanomami are not to be written off as merely aggressive people. They number about 9,000, one of the largest groups of forest living people in the world, but around 1,500 have died from disease, murder, poisoned rivers and invasion of their land.

The highland people of Papua New Guinea are even fiercer. The male initiation cult involves learning how to dominate women:

Inside the cult house, which no woman may enter, the Nama men store their sacred flutes whose sounds terrorize the women and children. Only male initiates learn that it is their fathers and brothers who make the sounds and not carnivorous supernatural birds. They swear to kill any woman or child who learns the secret even by accident . . . After being secluded in the cult house the initiates emerge into adulthood. They are given a bride whom they promptly shoot in the right thigh with an arrow to demonstrate unyielding power over her. Women work in the gardens, raise pigs, and do all the dirty work while men stand around gossiping, making speeches, and decorating themselves with paint, feathers and shells. (p.65)

The anthropologist David Gilmore has made a study of masculinity which confirms the prevalence of anxiety in the male; he has to show that he is able to perform. Gilmore (1990) describes a number of societies where maleness is valued highly in this way, including a study of Andalucian life, one of the places where the 'macho' concept was born. Here a man who has no children is a failure, but he also has to provide for his family. The breadwinning role, so challenged in our society, is actually one of the more durable and interesting roles for the man. This was what Margaret Mead (1962) regarded as the innovation of the human race, even if it turns out not to have been as indispensable as she thought. In a cash economy, breadwinning is actually a more important role than hunting in the foraging society, and Gilmore points out that it is fundamentally a generous, even sacrificial, thing to do – to make money and spend it on others. Manhood, he says, is a kind of male procreation. But it has to be seen to be done: 'a man's effectiveness is measured as others see him in action'. (p.35) So the performance does not have to be violent, domineering or humiliating to women, but it does have to be witnessed. This is, of course, what *testis* actually means: it is the evidence of manhood.

A Man's Place in the Modern World

Before we call for change in men, we will need to understand why we have resisted and hung on so doggedly for so long. This has to do with the fact that boys cannot become men without relinquishing their identification with their mothers (Greenson, 1968; Hudson and Jacot, 1991). The historical rise of patriarchy is really a slow version of what happens in the development of each boy in our Western societies.

At first, he is just a baby, and while his parents and others are keen to know which sex he is, he doesn't care one way or the other. So although he is treated differently from a baby girl, he is not conscious of the difference – he just loves his mummy. This can be compared with the prehistoric worship of goddesses and spirits.

Sometime during the second year he begins to sense the difference. This depends on being able to see the naked bodies of girls and boys, but also on the insistence of his caretakers that he is a boy, which is not like a girl. The girl is having complementary experiences while receiving the same sort of message: that is, that she is a girl, and not a boy. The difference is that she is surrounded by women, so she can see what she is meant to become (Phillips, 1993). The importance of this evidence is not diminished by the fact that many of the women seen by children now leave the house and go to work. This only increases the range of things women can be seen to be doing: looking after you, feeding you, doing household tasks, but also going out and coming back. Both boys and girls witness this, but the boy does not see much of the men. This is gradually changing, but the statistics exposing the new man's confidence trick are now well known: he claims to do his share, but he doesn't do as much as he says. In other words, it's a bit of a performance!

The boy is being told he is male, but sees vastly less of the male example than of the female. Logic dictates that if the male is different, then he must be unlike the female. The only thing to do is to give up everything to do with females and set off into the darkness to become one of those mysterious and powerful absent males. This is equivalent to the rise of the creator gods at the beginning of history. In order to feel male he has to jettison what he perceives as maternal qualities by putting mother down. As Jalmert (1990) says 'the positive outcome of this development is that the boy will see himself as separate with marked boundaries. The negative outcome is that the boy will have difficulties in getting close to other persons. We might even call it a fear of intimacy' (p.3). This sounds like a reasonable description of far too many men.

It does not have to be like that. If the man's place was, like the woman's, both in the home and out of it, then the boy would not have to grow up in this way. I do not mean that he will be able to avoid the negotiation of the delicate passage from dependent infant to assertive, gender-conscious toddler, but with adult males around him he can see for himself what he might become, and there would at once be more variety in his experience. Nor do I mean that men have to be the same as women (the inevitable segregations of sport will see to that!), but a greater range of identities and roles can become available for them, just as they are for modern women. For a child of either sex, a real man is so much more interesting than an absent fantasy, whatever exciting or important things he is meant to be doing. Notice that I say a '*real man*', a phrase normally reserved for one with particularly impressive powers, political, muscular or sexual. The trouble with that model, as we have seen, is that it implies putting women down.

Men as Partners

It should be clear enough that if we had a greater variety of couplings between men and women as parents, there would be a correspondingly greater variety of gender identities. This is particularly urgent now because of the imminent extinction of the 'old man', without any plausible successor waiting in the wings. Yet there is a great deal of anxiety about change because, whether we like it or not, it is happening now. The contortions of politicians trying to defend the old moral order is just one sign of widespread panic. This is nowhere more evident than in the threatened male, and his well-documented backlash. It is simply wrong to state that women's liberation has gone far enough when it has hardly started.

But the shrillness of the opposition to change must not be disregarded. What we may be witnessing is the beginning of the end of a really ancient patriarchal structure. How can this possibly happen without real fear on the part of men (and even women) everywhere, a fear which could produce further and ever-more desperate efforts to reassert authority? Either the frightened male is defeated, in which case the backlash will be all the more violent and possibly terminal, or he is taken on board as a thinking human being.

In order to do this, he will need to be brought up differently. We need to make a commitment to a more flexible male for the future. In spite of everything, there are many signs of change. Most men attend the delivery of their children now, compared with hardly any 30 years ago. But they still receive little social encouragement to participate as parents, even though we know that many men are now keen to do their share (Kraemer, 1994); or at least they say they are, which is a start. When they do, it increases the richness of the children's experience from infancy right up to adulthood (Lamb and Oppenheim, 1989; Russell and Radojevic, 1992; Pruett, 1993), but it would also make a difference to our expectations of men in general.

The man as engaged parent and marital partner is still far from the norm. Other chapters in this book examine the enormous challenges posed by other aspects of a real marriage partnership, where commitments of different kinds are made and kept. Most people still believe in this, which is why they go on getting married, even for the second and third time. Life away from home can be exciting for men, where they are free and feel less vulnerable. Yet that is not the whole story. Models of maleness in our society are terribly limited, although the fact that it is possible to write this now at all is evidence of real change. It could not have happened even 20 years ago. I do not underestimate the social and political changes necessary to allow men to participate in domestic life, but now is the time to push for it.

Sebastian Kraemer

11
Beyond the Couple

In 1899, Freud wrote in a letter to Fliess: 'I am accustoming myself to regarding every sexual act as an event between four individuals.' Freud was referring to his idea that bisexuality was a characteristic of each and every individual. Both boys and girls developed masculine and feminine identifications with both their mother and their father; the relative strength of each of these identifications determined the outcome of the Oedipal situation.

With the discovery of the unconscious, Freud postulated that the individual was not at the centre of her or himself: the ego is not the I. In addition to the ego, there are both the id and the super-ego. With his statement that the sexual act is an act between four individuals, Freud can be considered to be saying that *there is no such thing as a couple*. In psychoanalytic terms, this means that each individual has internalized the history of his or her identification with their primary relationships. Thus the very discipline which is supposed to represent one of the foundations of the individualistic universe, points out the social element in what most people would regard as a very private phenomena. The sexual act involves the story of two families, of two social groups.

Freud, especially in his later works, emphasized that individual psychology is from the outset simultaneously social psychology. He suggested that the prohibition of incest between parents and children represents the victory of the human order over the individual. His writings are therefore about the creation of this order and how it becomes separate from the biological order (Mitchell, 1984). Through the Oedipus Complex, the individual enters the symbolic order by establishing the differences between the sexes. The individual is not born but is constituted through sexual differentiation.

Anthropology, too, especially since the work of Lévi-Strauss (1969), has suggested that the incest taboo separates nature from culture, creating the symbolic order and establishing the distinction between the genders. This contrast between nature and culture must, however, be seen as an artificial creation of culture itself. There is no proof that a society has ever existed in which this taboo has not played a dominant role.

The incest taboo forces families to give up one of their members to other families, thus producing a system of exchange between them.

Lévi-Strauss pointed out that the minimal requirements of a kinship system included at least four types of family relations (1968):

- consanguinity, that is, a blood tie between a woman and her brother, who 'exchanged her';
- affinity (marriage);
- descent (between parents and children);
- avuncular relationships (between maternal uncle and mother's son); this relationship may also include other members of the mother's family of origin.

The fourth type of relationship is a reminder that for a couple to be created, the incest taboo requires the existence of a family that has given up one of its women. In Western societies this relationship is less important than in many traditional societies because the ideological stress is on the nuclear family. The arbitrary and social characteristics of the kinship system are thus concealed as the nuclear family is regarded as the 'natural', 'biological' form of family. This makes it difficult, and sometimes confusing, to assemble other types of family organizations into a classificatory system. The very word 'step family', for instance, suggests that it is a form that is replacing a 'real' family.

I think that many of the confusions one can identify in various attempts to classify different types of family forms are the result of a cultural system that emphasizes the nuclear family as a 'biological' and thus 'natural' form of family. The way in which culture shapes and values specific types of family forms is then lost. The distinction, in traditional societies, between 'cross' and 'parallel' cousins is, perhaps, an important illustration of my point that kinship classificatory systems are culturally determined, and, thus, arbitrary. Both types of cousins are children of siblings. Parallel cousins are cousins descending from siblings of the same sex (from father's brother or from mother's sister) and cross-cousins are children of siblings of opposite sexes (such as father's sister or mother's brother).

In many traditional societies, parallel cousins cannot marry and are designated by the same term as brothers and sisters, whereas marriage between cross-cousins is favoured. Lévi-Strauss (1969) has suggested that the distinction between parallel and cross-cousins is incompatible with Western biological concepts and is evidence of the eminently cultural aspect of kinship systems.

The interest of cross-cousins marriage lies especially in the fact that the division that it establishes between prescribed and prohibited spouses cuts across a category of relatives who, from the point of view of biological proximity, are strictly interchangeable. It points to the social origin of the incest taboo. (p.121–2)

My reason for emphasizing these points is to indicate how *culturally sensitive* one has to be towards the variety of family organizations. This is true from the outset, even when one is meeting a couple coming from an apparently similar cultural background to one's own. Feminist writings over recent decades have highlighted that men and women – by definition – bring as part of their personal luggage different emotional and sociological experiences. As the grandmother of one of the contributors to the book *Gender and Power in Families* (Perelberg and Miller, 1990) used to say, with a twinkle in her eye, whenever she heard about a man and a woman having marital difficulties: 'Well, everybody knows these mixed marriages [between a woman and a man] don't work.' (Jones, 1990)

I will develop the concept of *family map* to indicate the way in which it differs from, and relates to, that of culture. I will then outline a framework which connects the concepts of 'culture', 'family map', and 'patterns of interaction', and will consider the conceptual and clinical implications for helping couples and families.

Culture and Ethnicity

Most of the family therapy literature which has considered the cultural context in which families are placed has resulted from work with 'ethnic families' (e.g. McGoldrick *et al.*, 1982; Falicov, 1980). The most important result of this body of work has been the creation of background material relating to the range and diversity of ethnic groups in the United States. The fact that this interest in the notion of culture stems from work with 'exotic' families involves the implicit danger of associating culture with that which is unfamiliar. In contrast, what one is familiar with is naturalized and perceived as part of 'nature'.

The notion of culture is mostly perceived in general terms, as if cultures were monolithic entities sometimes defined within geographical boundaries – for example, the Irish, Germans, and Italians (Ablon, 1980), the Asians (Shon and Davis, 1982), the British (McGill and Pearce, 1982), and the Italians (Rotunno and McGoldrick, 1982). Internal differentiations, in terms of social class, social stratifications or lifestyles are generally ignored

Conceptual Framework

A number of concepts will be useful in establishing the connections between culture, family and patterns of behaviour.

First, one should consider the *level of meaning* as well as the behavioural and emotional characteristics of *patterns of interaction*. It is this level that reminds the observer that it is not possible, through observation alone, to understand that which is being observed. This is particularly obvious when one is dealing with the exotic. For instance, if an Englishman goes to Africa and sees a man using a knife to scar an adolescent while a group of observers dance and sing, he might recognize the event as ritual, although its full meaning could not be fully comprehended until placed in the context of the specific culture to which it belonged.

When dealing with the 'exotic', one is reminded that the rules of everyday life which are taken for granted are not, in fact, a 'given' part of the natural world, but are the product of a specific culture. In daily life these rules are so internalized that we are very rarely led to think about them. There exist, nevertheless, certain moments which force us to do this. To take an example, Bunuel's film *The Phantom of Liberty* vividly denaturalized and thus made the viewer aware of the cultural origins of social rules. In one of the scenes in this film, a family receives some guests, who immediately sit around what we would perceive as a dining table. But instead of chairs, they sit on lavatories while making conversation, smoking and reading newspapers. When a little girl complains that she is hungry, her mother reprimands her by reminding her that the subject should not be talked about at the table. One of the guests then excuses himself and retires to a small room at the end of the corridor – the equivalent of a toilet – and locks the door in order to eat in privacy. Thus, the film inverts patterns of everyday life in Western societies so that eating is transformed into a private and polluted event, whereas excreting becomes a social and public activity. Every object in the scene is familiar but the change of context creates the changed meaning. The perception of arbitrariness is also facilitated when one's habitual way of thinking is disrupted. Crises are situations in which the rules which underlie family life can be thought about, possibly causing them to be changed or reinforced.

Second, the concepts of *social structure and social organization* (Firth, 1969) are useful mediators between the concept of culture on the one hand, and that of patterns of interaction on the other. They stand respectively for form and process. Social organization implies concrete social activity which is arranged in sequences. Social structure is a conceptual, not an operational or descriptive tool. Both are functions of the culture. Here function is defined as that which establishes a relationship of interdependence (Bateson, 1958). The concept of culture lies at a higher level of abstraction than 'social structure' and 'social organization' and neither of the latter two concepts can be derived from the former solely by deduction.

Third, there is the concept of *family map*. Such a map, I suggest, is the set of ideas which guides behaviour and emotions in everyday life, which organizes and systematizes the world, and transforms its sensory dimensions into intelligible ones. Such a map establishes boundaries and shapes on otherwise undifferentiated territory. Family maps are a function of culture, social structure and organization but, once again, cannot be derived directly from any of these, since maps involve a specific practice within the family. This implies the existence of specific configurations (shapes) within couples and families. A family map may contain contradictory ideas and principals at different stages of the lifecycle held by different members in the family. An example of contradictory values might be that of a Hindu family which emigrated to England 16 years ago. The parental couple could still guide their lives according to the belief systems by which they had been brought up. The children, by contrast, may be more in touch with the belief systems they learn about at school. The family map would contain the conflicting ideas and expectations held by the two generations (Spiegel, 1957).

The concept of family map cuts across any notion of a dichotomy between family and society as it allows for the presence of contradictory meanings. It emphasizes both the specificity of the family and its *articulation* to the wider society.

It is possible to identify specific points of reference from which types of family maps can be traced. I will outline two models which lie at two extremes of a continuum. I have designated these types of family maps as *hierarchical* and *symmetrical*. Hierarchical families are characterized by segregated activities and role relationships, while activities and relationships of symmetrical families are shared and termed joint (Bott, 1957). These differences in family structure have implications for the patterning of behaviour and emotions within the couple and between the parents and their children.

Family maps can be derived from the following points of reference:

- the way in which activities within the home are organized along gender and generational lines (Bott, 1957);

- the connections which the couple maintain with their networks of friends and relatives (Bott, 1957);
- partners' attitudes to their children (Bernstein, 1974);
- the ways in which family members perceive the connection between the individual and the world around them, in other words, whether they emphasize the autonomy of the individual (an egocentric model) or the role of the individual in relation to other family members (a sociocentric model). This will have an implication for the pattern of intimacy within the family (Firth, 1969).

In terms of the relationship between gender roles, the hierarchical couple is characterized by strict segregation of tasks. The woman is responsible for the bulk of the domestic work, which is strongly identified with femininity. The man will only do tasks, such as gardening or decorating, which are regarded as suitably male. The mother takes charge of most of the everyday care of the children, even though both parents are considered to be responsible for their socialization and the inculcation of moral values. The father tends to be more distant towards the children and more frequently absent from home. Even in symmetrical couples, where the father is generally more closely involved with the children, intimacy tends to be confined to certain limited activities (Newson and Newson, 1963, 1970, 1976; Perelberg, 1983; Lewis and O'Brien, 1987).

Although in symmetrical couples the fathers are fairly closely involved in the educational and moral aspects of child rearing, they are also often aware of the difficulty of sharing the activities of child care (such as bathing, feeding, changing nappies) equally and feel that these remain predominantly in the woman's sphere. The activities of child care seem to be the last sphere that men share with women, even in symmetrical families.

Symmetrical families emphasize the sharing of household tasks and child-rearing activities, and the ideal is one of equality in the conjugal partnership. Among these families, greater stress is placed on the importance of women having independent careers. Hierarchical families emphasize the positional relationship of members of the family: roles and moral rules are stressed, and individuals refer constantly to their respective roles by stating for example, 'You will do this because I say so, and I am your father and you are my daughter.' Hierarchical families are composed of persons defined in terms of their position or role in the system, whereas in symmetrical families the emphasis is on the autonomy and uniqueness of each individual. These two types of families are associated with two types of networks. Hierarchical families have tight-knit networks, whereas those of symmetrical families are looser and more disparate.

Table 8: Types of Family Maps

	Hierarchical	Symmetrical
Unit of analysis	The person (roles): socio-centric model. The biological individual is more clearly embedded in a wider network of social relationships.	The autonomous individual: egocentric model.
Role-relationship	Segregated	Joint
Perception of children	Roles stressed	Individual qualities stressed
Network	Close-knit	Loose-knit

These two models, hierarchical and symmetrical, do not deny the empirical diversity of family forms, but are constructs which suggest that several variables must be considered in any attempt to identify specific patterns of family organization and family maps (Bernstein, 1974; Edgell, 1980; Rapaport *et al.*, 1982). Establishing structural principles for identifying family maps cannot be equated with creating descriptive categories, such as nuclear, one-parent or extended families. These merely describe phenomena rather than establish their organizing principles. A one-parent family, for instance, could be either hierarchical or symmetrical depending on the points of reference which constitute its map.

At this point, it is possible to draw the conceptual framework which establishes the links between the various levels of analysis: culture, social structure, social organization, family maps (ranging from hierarchical to symmetrical), and patterns of interaction (which must include the level of meaning because it most clearly refers back to the existence of family maps).

An hierarchical relationship exists between these various levels. If one moves from patterns of interaction towards the concept of culture, one is moving towards a higher level of abstraction. Each level is a function of all the others in that there exists a relationship

Table 9: Conceptual Framework Establishing Links Between the Various Levels of Analysis

Culture
(an attempt to establish coherence)

Social Structure
(form taken by historical and sociological relationships)

Social Organization
(process)

Family Maps
(set of ideas which guide behaviour and emotion in everyday life)

Patterns of Interaction
(transactions between biological individuals
which involve behaviour, emotion and meaning)

of interdependence, but none can be deduced from any of the others, as there is always a new dimension to be added. Greater attention must be paid to the diversity of specific processes and events when one moves towards patterns of interaction and, conversely, moving towards the concept of culture involves the integration of additional analytic concepts.

I will now turn to the relevance of these issues for helping families change. Three illustrations are offered from my clinical practice. All the names and identifying details about the families have been altered in order to protect their privacy.

The Stepford Wife: The Masters

The Masters were referred by their doctor because of Mrs Master's continuing depression, for which she had recently been prescribed antidepressants. The couple had two children in late adolescence, and the whole family were invited to come to the first session. In many ways they were typical of so many families in which the woman presents herself as being depressed. Mr Master was prepared to talk about his wife's depression, about when it had started, and the various therapies they had tried. While relating this sequence, he analysed his wife, criticized her and patronized her, always using a very sensible tone of voice. Mrs Master basically smiled and nodded in agreement. The children remained on the periphery of the conversation.

The therapist spent much of the session finding out about the family, their life together and their aspirations for the future. The children were perceived as letting their parents down by having chosen lifestyles completely different from them. John had recently decided he was homosexual, and Mary was having an affair with a much older married man. The channels of communications between the two generations were blocked. Mr Master spoke in a very rational manner about his children being different from them, telling his wife she would have to accept the situation. The therapist pointed out that they were all concerned about hurting each other by expressing their feelings, and that Mrs Master, in particular, felt she had to shut up for fear of further alienating her children.

When the therapist explored the connections with the previous generation, the closeness between Mrs Master and her mother became clear. Whenever she felt she was too depressed, she went to stay with her mother for a few days until she felt better. Mr Master, on his side, had severed contact with his own parents. Throughout that session the therapist formulated the problem so that it involved three generations. One of the main interventions, however, addressed the relationship between the husband and the wife. The therapist asked the family if they had seen the film *The Stepford Wives*. In the film, which is set in a small town in America, a group of husbands replace their wives with robots which are in every way like their wives, except that they always look immaculate and do everything the husbands want them to do; most specifically, they nod at everything their husbands do and say. Mrs Master, too, nodded and smiled at everything her husband said.

The whole family had seen the film, and remembered the actors in it. They were intrigued by the comparison with themselves. Mr Master, however, started to say how difficult it was to get Mrs Master to say what she thought. The therapist suggested the answer to that problem might lie in the previous generation, and invited them to ask Mrs Master's parents to come to the next session. Mrs Master responded by saying it was the most mind-blowing suggestion she had ever heard!

Mr and Mrs Brown (Mrs Master's parents) came to the next session. The new information that came out of this session was Mrs Master's fear of her father, and Mr Master's fear of both his parents-in-law. Mrs Master talked about how much she had always needed her father's approval and advice. In the session she was challenged to tell her father about her ideas. The difficulty throughout was finding somebody who would be able to help her to do so. Mr Master was not able to help her, partly because the rules of his own family of origin stated that parents could not be challenged. One had either to conform or leave.

The task was left to Mrs Brown, who then expressed the feeling that throughout her life she had fulfilled the role of switchboard in her family. Communication between her husband and her children had always been routed through her. The therapist acknowledged that the family had given Mrs Brown that role, and that she, herself, had felt she was responsible for working out the relationships in the family. A crucial aspect of this rule for the women, was that while father and daughter could not talk directly to each other, mother and daughter were bound together. The paradox was that Mrs Master, on her side, believed that in the final analysis she had to be there for any conversation to take place between her mother and her father. By helping her daughter to talk to her father, Mrs Brown was challenging this belief that she (Mrs Brown) was afraid of her husband, and was strong enough to handle him. Mr Brown, in turn, was being challenged to engage more fully in his relationship with both his daughter and his wife.

The therapist's perception of gender roles and the dominant expectations about them in the wider society was central to these interventions. In the first session Mrs Master's depression was reframed in terms of her not being able to speak in a relationship she experienced as biased towards her husband. They were *both* challenged, however, by the intervention. During subsequent sessions it became clear that Mr Master perceived his wife as inaccessible. Mrs Master's 'depression' was thus a 'solution' to a complicated set of issues in that it attempted to 'freeze' the conflicts within relationships in the family. The relationship between the couple was embedded in a wider family network that needed to be understood for the therapy to be able to take place.

Three Generational Parenthood: The Donalds

The Donalds were referred for help because of Debbie's continuing refusal to attend school, her unhappiness and lack of friends, and the recurrent abdominal pains that she experienced. Debbie came to the first session in tears, with her parents. It became clear that the composition of the family was complex. Although they lived in the same house with their three children – Sylvia (20), Robert (18) and

Debbie (13) – Mr and Mrs Donald (72 and 42, respectively) no longer slept together; they had 'separated'. They shared the same house with Mrs Donald's new partner, Mr O'Hara (22) and their three children, Gemma (5), Jo (4) and Sarah (2). All of them were invited to attend subsequent interviews.

The Donalds presented their family map as that of a 'democratic', undifferentiated unit in which everyone had an equal right to express their point of view. The fact that the criterion of age, for instance, was not important in terms of ranking was indicated by the ages of Mr Donald, Mrs Donald and Mr O'Hara. In the first session, as they reluctantly told me about the composition of their household, Mr and Mrs Donald were also testing my reaction. When my response was simply to invite everybody to come to the next session in order to help Debbie more effectively, they immediately saw that I was not taking a moral stance. Nevertheless, they were clearly on their guard.

At this stage, the fact that I was both an anthropologist and a foreigner was of immense help. Because I was a foreigner they could assume that I did not know how uncommon their household arrangements might be, and as an anthropologist I had been trained to be aware of the diversity of lifestyles. I therefore accepted their decision to be a three-parent family living in the same household and recognized their family map in which both the autonomy of each individual and joint activities were emphasized.

Gradually, I reached a basic agreement with the family. At that specific moment in time something was making Debbie unhappy. The family would have to help me find out what it was, and in order to do so, latent rules of family life would have to be clarified even though, in normal everyday life, the rules need not be articulated. I also said, at that stage, that all societies had at least two principle differentiations: sex and age (La Fontaine, 1978). The latter, in particular, seemed to me to be rather ambiguous in their family. The strategic component of the therapeutic contract with the family was that while I respected the idiosyncratic, loose, three-parent family organization which was consciously chosen by the family, I should also reach agreement about the notions of gender, hierarchy and boundaries between the generations.

Throughout the therapy a tension was maintained between the notions of the family as a democratic unit and those of boundaries and hierarchies. My hypothesis was that as Sylvia, Debbie's elder sister, was about to leave home, Debbie was placed in an ambiguous position. She was, on the one hand, Mr and Mrs Donald's daughter, that is, she was one of the children in the household. On the other hand, the existence of Mr and Mrs Donald as a parental couple implied that either Mr O'Hara was one of the children, or that he was available as a possible partner for Debbie. This ambiguity was increased by Mrs Donald's feelings of incompetence in looking after the home and the three smaller children, and her constant request for help from Debbie. By not going to school, Debbie was staying in the house and taking over from her mother. She also helped to maintain the balance between the two families. While she was at home, Mr Donald still retained a role, since they had all decided in the past that it was better to live together for the sake of the children.

Potentially they all had something to lose if Debbie got better. The crucial aspect of the therapeutic process required the acceptance of the three-parent family structure within the same household, at the same time as boundaries were being traced between parents and children, mother and daughter, around all the siblings, and then around older and younger siblings.

The Family Business: The Sumas

This family comprised a mother, father and nine children (five girls and four boys, between 32 and 16 years old). My first contact with them was through a telephone call from their eldest, 32-year-old daughter, Simena, saying that her 24-year-old brother, Sunjae, had become mute and refused to get up in the morning. She asked for an appointment, which the parents and seven of the nine children attended.

The Sumas were Hindus, East African Asians, who had come to England for political reasons having had to flee from their home country while leaving all their property and money behind. When they arrived in this country they were helped by Mrs Suma's brother to open a business. Mr Suma started to drink heavily. The four eldest sisters took charge of the business and the older brother went to college. The father, therefore, had completely lost his position as the provider for the family. There had been conflicts between husband and wife who had decided not to speak to each other again. They had not spoken to each other for some 12 years before they came to the session. To have changed this situation would have involved 'loss of face' for each of them.

During the two years prior to the session the following events had taken place in rapid succession. The third sister married and emigrated to America. The fourth sister left the family business to marry a Muslim. The father had been very upset by this and had stopped speaking to her. This sister was also not on speaking terms with the two sisters still involved in the business. The 31-year-old daughter was about to get married, leaving Simena, the eldest, to look after the 'family business' on her own. The business, a grocery shop, was located on the other side of London, where she lived on her own. At the weekends she went back to the family home. Two years previously Sunjae had become involved with a Muslim guru who had converted him to Islam. He had been told by his parents to go and live with Simena because they thought that by looking after the family business he might 'become himself again'.

During the first session, two versions of Sunjae's problems were put forward. The father definitely thought Sunjae should see a psychiatrist as he had become 'kinky' after his contact with the guru. According to the second version, there was a communication problem within the family and Sunjae, because he was so sensitive, was more vulnerable than the others. The three older children supported this view and wanted to employ me to get the parents to talk to each other.

My hypothesis was derived from looking at the family map. This was a hierarchical family with segregated role-relationships where, due to historical circumstances and their specific life history, the relationships between the genders and the generations had become inverted. The women had taken over the task of providing for the family and the children that of looking after their parents. At that specific moment in the lifecycle, Simena was at risk of remaining, for ever, the only one responsible for looking after the business, her parents, and Sunjae.

Silence had been used by the family to deal with major contradictions. These included the inversion of positions between the sexes and the generations. The mother and the father had stopped speaking to each other after coming to England and the fourth daughter was not speaking to the family because of her marriage to a Muslim. By becoming silent in his sister's house, Sunjae attempted to activate the most powerful person in the family – who also had most to lose at that point in time – to try and do something about the situation. Simena, in fact, had persistently tried to talk to each parent about Sunjae's problem, but because they could not talk to each other she became a prisoner of her role as mediator. By the end of the first session I realized that to agree that there was a 'communication problem' in the family would only further alienate Mr Suma. I decided to support his position and asked a psychiatrist to see Sunjae.

His diagnosis was that there was nothing psychiatrically wrong with Sunjae, and this gave added impetus to our meetings. I accepted the father's idea that the guru had made Sunjae 'kinky' and proceeded to ask the family to discuss with Sunjae whether he was at that point Hindu or Muslim. It turned out that no one was sure of the answer. I labelled Sunjae's silence as an expression of the fact that he did not know who he was. I asked whether they knew of any ceremony which would allow a Muslim to become a Hindu again, in case Sunjae wanted to go through it. Mr Suma turned out to be the only person in the family who was knowledgeable about religious matters. During the following session, Sunjae discussed with his father his possible re-conversion to Hinduism. The conversations went on for weeks, and then Mr Suma organized a ceremony which Sunjae underwent a few months later. Throughout the process the therapist never asked that the mother and the father should talk to each other directly. The men in the family had their role reinstated and this allowed Simena greater flexibility and freedom from her previously rigid position.

The therapeutic interventions required careful tracking of the family map. While this included the observation of patterns of interaction in the room (the mother and the father not speaking to each other, Simena acting as mediator between the two, the father being largely ignored in the first session and so on), what these meant to the family had also to be considered. The interventions which followed were then syntonic with the principles of the family map.

It is clear that the concept of culture would not have been sufficient to understand what was happening within this family. There was a dynamic process taking place in which roles and rules were being redefined and renegotiated. The new arrangements did not necessarily 'fit' either those predominant in their traditional context or those of the new setting, but the concept of a family map allowed the dynamics of the process to be considered.

This chapter has introduced the family map as a concept that mediates between the family, the couple and the culture to which it belongs. Although maps are always present in the encounters between therapists and their couples or families, it is only when faced with 'exotic' families that the therapist becomes aware of their existence. I suggest this concept should be brought to the centre of the conceptual framework of couple and family therapy.

I have also suggested a conceptual framework for the analysis of the links between family and culture by defining and indicating the connections between the concepts of culture, social structure, social organization, hierarchical and symmetrical types of family maps, and patterns of interaction. The proposed conceptual framework indicates an hierarchical relationship of successively higher levels of abstraction leading from 'patterns of interaction' towards the concept of 'culture'. Each level is a function of all the others (and all are interdependent) but none can be deduced from knowledge of any of the others as a new dimension must always be added.

The risk faced by marital and family therapists is that of attempting to *colonize* those who seek this help by attempting to reconstruct family patterns without concerning themselves with the meanings which are attributed to lifestyles. The diversity of social contexts is then reduced to pathological structures. If couples exist only in culture, meaning can be attributed only through language; the understanding of a specific pattern cannot be achieved through observation or logical inference alone. It is necessary to ask the individual members of a family about their perception of what they are doing so that their meanings can be taken into consideration. What family members say and do, and even their unconscious structures, are, in the final analysis, derived from, and only exist within, the symbolic systems at their disposal.

Rosine Jozef Perelberg

12
Marriage: a New Millennium?

The dimension of time is perhaps one of the strangest of symbolic systems in its effects upon human behaviour. Our lives are structured by time so that when familiar routines change we feel disorientated, out of sorts and not quite ourselves. Time-frames provide definition for our lives in the present. An absence of them creates a sense of anomie – ask anyone who has recently lost their job.

Our sense of time past defines who we are as people. It tells us where we have come from and provides a framework within which history and biography – the collective and personal stories that tell ourselves and others about our identity – are worked out. Anniversaries carry importance because they remind us of what has gone before; they create opportunities to celebrate achievements and to take stock for the future. Our sense of the time we have left for us fashions our images of the future – it shapes our fantasies, and we seek to define it either in terms of what has already been, or in diametric opposition to the past.

We believe that time changes everything, but we often act today exactly as we did yesterday. While living in an age of accelerating technological change, we can still hold on to the conviction that 'plus ça change, plus c'est la même chose'. The present is no more than the convergence of our remembered (and unremembered) past and our expected future, creating a line of continuity that can sometimes elude us as we peer myopically in both directions.

So perhaps it is unsurprising that we approach the close not only of this century but also of the second millennium with a mixture of apprehension and excitement as we take stock of what is happening around us. Marriage does not escape our critical gaze as we seek to predict what is to come from what has gone before. The millennium invites review of how marriage has grown from its roots in the Judaeo-Christian tradition (see Chapter 3); it is a kind of wedding anniversary with which a base metal or precious stone has yet to be identified. What *is* precious about marriage has been called into question. Despite the caution advised in Chapter 1, statistical trends have been used to argue that marriage is an outdated institution. And the reason most usually given is that the institution fails to reflect changing aspirations in the relationships between men and women. So, the argument runs, it is not people who are unfit for marriage, but marriage that is unfit for people; round pins cannot be expected to fit into square holes.

The historical dimensions of this book span a very short period of time, concentrating on marriage in the second half of this century, and occasionally casting a backwards look over the past 100 or 200 years. Yet the tension between the personal aspirations of people in their love relations and the social buttressing of marriage is evident throughout; the dilemma about people conforming to marriage or marriage being tailored to people is one that is not confined to the closing decades of the twentieth century. In 1791 Samuel Johnson diagnosed the ineptitude of people as the root cause of unhappy marriage and prescribed arrangement as the solution:

I believe marriages would in general be as happy, and often more so, if they were all made by the lord chancellor, upon due consideration of the character and circumstances, without the parties having any choice in the matter. (Mooney, 1989)

Just over 60 years later John Stuart Mill, who wanted to live with Harriet Taylor but realized it would be socially impossible outside marriage, saw the institution itself as being the problem and was moved to write a formal disclaimer on the grounds that

. . . the whole character of the marriage relation as constituted by law [is] such as both she and I conscientiously disapprove, for this amongst other reasons, that it confers upon one of the parties to the contract, legal power and control over the person, property, and freedom of action of the other party, independent of her own wishes and will. (Mooney, 1989)

Behind this dilemma lies a fundamental question about the purpose of marriage. The established Church of England has had no difficulty over the years defining what marriage is for, although there has been a significant reordering of priorities (Sadgrove, 1993). Whereas the 1662 *Book of Common Prayer* identified the 'procreation of children', 'a remedy against sin' (the regulation of sexual behaviour) and 'mutual society, help and comfort' as the three functions of marriage, the 1980 *Alternative Service Book* reverses the order and changes the language to emphasize the importance of marriage as a relationship:

Marriage is given, that husband and wife may comfort and help each other, living faithfully together in need and plenty, in sorrow and in joy. It is given, that with delight and tenderness they may know each other in love, and through their bodily union, may strengthen the union of their hearts and lives. It is given, that they may have children and be blessed in caring for them . . .

At different times in history, different importance has been given to the private and public aspects of marriage, and for different reasons. I want to suggest four processes that describe and are relevant to our understanding of modern marriage, and to recapitulate some of the paradoxes and contradictions that are contained within it. The processes can be described as *the privatization of marriage, the pursuit of an egalitarian dream, the decline of absolute values and the rise of relativism,* and *the shift from rights to responsibilities.* None of these processes is self-contained; each interlocks with the others.

The Privatization of Marriage

There can be no clearer indications of the pressure to deregulate marriage than falling marriage rates and the rising popularity of cohabitation as a prelude if not an alternative to marriage. Three in every five women marrying for the first time are already living with their husband-to-be. Almost a half of all conceptions take place outside marriage, and one in every three births are to unmarried women (nearly three-quarters of these being registered by both parents). The trend is not peculiar to the UK, but is evident in other European countries.

Attitude surveys over the past forty years also suggest there has been a change of values with regard to marriage. The social position it afforded, the valuing of men as providers and women as home-makers, has been succeeded by assessments of marriage in relational terms. Mutual respect, fidelity, understanding, tolerance and a happy sexual relationship are rated more highly than the practicalities of an adequate income, good housing, and sharing household chores – or having similar religious beliefs, social backgrounds and political views. There is agreement between men and women across European countries on these ratings which emphasize the private companionate aspects of marriage over the public functional institution. There is also a broad measure of agreement in the UK on attitudes that support people living together outside marriage, although most (and especially among the older age groups) would advise marriage if a couple was planning to have children.

A consistency of attitudes is matched by a consistency in the kinds of problems that attend them. The privatization of marriage, into 'companionate' arrangements (see Chapter 5), or 'symmetrical family maps' (see Chapter 11) means that couples have to be more self-sufficient than their 'hierarchically' structured counterparts in meeting the range of practical and emotional needs that arise for the partners. Marriage then becomes what Bott (1971) describes as a 'pressure cooker' in which couples are expected to move in and out of the roles of lover, best friend, adviser, colleague, parent, sibling, in-law and so on. In other cultures, in other circumstances, an array of people might be expected to play some of these parts. This compression of 'external' relationships into the couple forum is matched by an articulation of 'internal' object relationships that populate marriage with 'unconscious phantasies' (see Chapter 4). It is interesting to speculate that these phantasies might be less disturbing to the couple if there was a wider network of family members in relation to whom they could find expression.

While women and men agree upon the importance of emotional support and companionship in marriage, women are much more likely than men to feel disappointed in this respect – three times more likely, if a Gallup poll commissioned in 1990 is to be believed. Taking the filing of petitions of divorce as a yardstick, women are also three times more likely than men to lead the way out of marriage. Whether the problem is that women expect too much of marriage or men deliver too little, one explanation for the current instability of marriage is suggested by the figures: the thwarting of companionate expectations of the couple's relationship, resulting in a burden of intolerable disappointment which, unmitigated, leads ultimately to the irretrievable breakdown of marriage.

Where are the safety valves to ensure the build-up of pressure in marriage finds release? As marriage becomes a private affair there are fewer social reference points for couples to check out their experiences against those of others. There are also fewer socially recognized boundaries and rituals to help them take up their new roles and to provide them with a degree of protection and support. The couple has to be self-reliant from the outset. If things go wrong, it can be easy to believe that the reasons are purely personal, with all the feelings of anger, guilt, shame and failure that can attend such a judgement. Consequently, it becomes harder for partners to talk to each other and to those around them about what is going on in their relationship. Privatized marriage is the hardest kind of marriage to help: couples are reluctant to disclose their problems; others are reluctant to intrude.

The little we know about cohabitation does not suggest it as an arrangement that overcomes the problems of contemporary marriage. Longterm cohabiting relationships may be patterned on the same basis as marriage itself, and subject to as many, if not more, pressures with fewer safeguards. One of the interesting outcomes of McRae's (1993) study of 330 cohabiting mothers was the indication that marriage retained its practical value as an economic contract. Many of the mothers in her sample were not well off, had few assets to hand on, and were relatively ignorant about the relationship between cohabiting status and parental rights and responsibilities in law. While women complained of the high cost of weddings, a fear of divorce and a disregard for marriage, this was not likely to be a longterm deterrent to marriage for those with material resources to safeguard. For those who had no such resources marriage might seem irrelevant, but their chosen alternative structured considerable uncertainty into their living arrangements and increased the likelihood of their needing state aid.

Pursuing the Egalitarian Dream

The economics of marriage focus attention on both the domestic economy of the home and the world of paid employment. When the social history of the Western world in the second half of this century comes to be written, the chances are that the women's movement is likely to emerge as the most significant theme. Insofar as marriage has served a social function through institutionalizing a gender-based division of labour to provide answers to two pressing questions about social organization – *Who will pay for dependants?* (men), and *Who will care for them?* (women) – it represents a somewhat tarnished receptacle for the heady brew of egalitarianism expected, if not achieved, by contemporary couples. While earning activities continue to be valued very much more highly than caring activities, and the demarcation between the two is drawn principally in terms of gender, patriarchal aspects of the institution of marriage are no longer tenable. But, change is afoot – in terms of economic, relational and emotional labour.

On the economic front there has been a marked increase over recent decades in the number of married women in paid employment. In England, to take but one example, the proportion of married women in employment who have children under ten years old is now three in every four. The number of women entering higher education has grown substantially in the post-war period, too, although this is not always reflected in subsequent career outcomes.

Changing practices reflect changing attitudes; changing attitudes reflect changing practices. The European Commission's rolling programme of research on attitudes has noted that married men are now more accepting of married women working than they were even ten years ago, the more so the younger and better educated they are. There have also been shifts in attitudes about the kind of work it is proper for women to do. The old conundrum of the boy injured in a car accident in which his father was killed, being admitted to hospital and the operating theatre only for the surgeon to say 'Someone else must operate, this is my boy,' should not now puzzle us for very long. There is growing acceptance of women working as surgeons, bus drivers, soldiers on active service and in other roles that traditionally have been regarded as the exclusive preserve of men. Within the European Community, Denmark is the country with the most egalitarian attitudes, where the ideal is that women and men should both be employed and share household and child-rearing responsibilities. Ireland is the most traditional of the European countries in terms of attitudes that support segregated spheres of activities between the sexes. Interestingly, in both Denmark and Ireland there is a high degree of agreement about the roles of men and women, unlike some of the mid-range countries where women are likely to want the egalitarian option and men are less sure. It is also interesting to note that in 1970, traditional roles were favoured in Denmark as well.

It is one thing to espouse egalitarian principles, quite another to put them into practice. While women are a growing part of the work force, many are employed in the lower-paid sectors of the economy and in part-time jobs. Women are frequently paid less than men for the same job, they have less security at work, more interrupted career paths and hence fewer entitlements (see Chapter 8).

A reality that has, perhaps, yet to sink in is that the working world of men is also changing. Handy (1989) points out that of the 26 million at work in Britain, only 17.5 are in full-time employment, and this proportion is falling. The emerging pattern of corporate life is what he describes as the 'Shamrock' organization. The first leaf of this organization is a small, professional core of staff undertaking activities that are essential to the business and, operating on the principle of subsidiarity, putting out to tender everything that it is not essential for them to do. The second leaf is composed of specialist sub-contractors who, in turn, are likely to have a large contractual fringe. The third leaf is a flexible labour force of part-time, temporary workers responding to peaks and troughs in the demand for their services. Handy suggests that this particular Shamrock might have a fourth leaf: the customers themselves, who pick their own, make their own, assemble their own and so on – all activities that used to involve paid work provided by an employer.

Technology is reducing the demand for labour, revolutionizing our concept of work and changing the nature of the work place (some estimate that one-quarter of the work force will be operating from home at the turn of the century). With both women and men being available for work, and technology reducing jobs, there is a crisis ahead, especially for those in manual and unskilled occupations. The danger aspect of this crisis is that half the world will work double time and half not at all, resulting in a mutually envious society divided into the 'haves' and the 'have nots'. Even for those with work, employment will not provide the conditions of security that it once did. There are no longer 'jobs for life'.

The opportunity aspect of the crisis is to tailor work to life, rather than the other way round. This holds the possibility of opening choices for men and women, extending their sense of being in control of their own lives.

What has any of this to do with marriage? Well, quite a lot, really. Not only has the telephone, fax and word processor redefined geographical boundaries between home and work, not only does unemployment impose material, territorial and status problems for couples, but also there is a glaring gap in the market: there are too few people to undertake the caring functions of society. With the resource of additional time there are real opportunities to re-think gender-defined relationships between men and women and address the twin monsters undermining the stability of family life as identified by Richard Jolly in his address to the opening conference of the International Year of the Family in 1993: the *apartheid of gender* which overburdens men and oppresses women, and the *poverty of affluence* which reduces the time working parents can spend with their children. The choice for couples is between a more balanced and flexible approach to child-rearing and family care responsibilities, or buying in services from outside. If marriage is a Shamrock organization, couples must decide what are the principal functions of marriage and which, under the principle of subsidiarity, can be contracted out to other people.

These questions need to be considered in relation to the gendered division of relational and emotional labour addressed in Chapters 9 and 10. The political assault on welfare and dependency has echoes of the ambivalence that can be experienced at a personal level in relation to those upon whom we depend and who depend upon us. Placing the filter of gender into this equation results in images of women as both dependent on and depended upon by men, and images of men as independent of and dependent on women. Add a distorting filter, and the images depict women as only dependent on men and men as always being depended on by women.

The developmental explanation for the distortions that exist in the way needs are managed and feelings expressed between men and women is to be found in the archetypal figure of the mother, who excites fear and longing in both women and men. Despite this common experience of having been wholly in the hands of a mother powerful enough to determine life and death, parenting arrangements are structured in ways that result in ambivalent feelings being managed in quite distinct ways between the sexes. Women are brought up by and with their mothers at home, and are unconsciously taught to put the needs of others before their own. This provides the parameters within which emotional needs must be satisfied. One outcome can be that women live vicariously, looking after the needs of others in order that they might be looked after themselves (Eichenbaum and Orbach, 1983). Men, on the other hand, grow up by leaving their mothers and joining their (often domestically absent) fathers in the world outside. Independence and achievement is valued here, and this sets the parameters for how men set about meeting their emotional needs.

Central to the argument is the conception of women as immensely powerful creative beings, envied and feared by men who are exiled from their world and who, in response, seek to diminish and devalue their power. Women collude with the phantasy that they depend on men and must subject themselves insofar as they fear the consequences of breaking the umbilical tie with 'mother' and becoming independent of her, and to the extent that she represents the female world. This is a psychological argument, explaining a process that operates subtly and, often, unconsciously, and one that can unfold in the therapeutic discourse (see Chapter 4). What binds women and men together in phantasy is the fear that if women use their power – or even acknowledge it – they will destroy men, so men must be protected.

A central question invited by this train of thought is how far the aspirations towards companionate marriage and equal opportunities can be secured without children experiencing women working outside the home as well as inside, men working inside the home as well as outside, and the two co-operating in the organization of both spheres of life?

But how easy it would be to substitute one orthodoxy with another. What new monsters might then be introduced?

The Decline of Absolute Values and the Rise of Relativism

Certainties, in the field of human relations, as elsewhere have enormous appeal, but they tend not to last for long. When change is rapid and 'discontinuous' (Handy, 1989), past certainties no longer provide a reliable guide to the future. The changing roles of men and women, the impact of technology on working practices, the disconnection of child-rearing from marriage and the challenges issuing from unprecedented levels of divorce all constitute changes that appear discontinuous from the perspective of a human lifetime. They also constitute a substantial personal and social agenda for the new millennium. The work on this agenda is already taking place behind the net-curtained worlds of domestic life, and with greater and lesser degrees of success. In this process, couples must rely heavily on their personal resources, for there are few social reference points to chart the way. Often there is a reluctance to seek out social pointers for fear of invoking the dual standards of a past era to deal with the uncertainties of the present. People are not always sure of the basics they want to get back to.

Some evidence of the shift away from absolute values can be found in the declining influence of religion as a belief system, code of conduct and expression of conviction. In the ascendant are counselling and therapeutic activities, which exist to help people discover personal meaning from their own experience. The quest for meaning is, of course, a spiritual activity, and I believe the institutions of religion and therapy have much in common – including, sometimes, a propensity to generate dogma. One difference I perceive is that therapeutic activities aim to help people discover and review the values and assumptions which derive from their individual life experience and guide their behaviour in relationships. In that sense, the truth that is sought after is a relative truth; the authority for it is personal and individual. In contrast, the values of religion are essentially collective and absolute; authority derives from a personal resonance with received truth which is shared by a community of believers.

The differences may be more apparent than real. A resonance between inner and outer realities is the foundation of meaning in religious and therapeutic activities. A belief in the power of the unseen and the invisible applies at least as much to psychoanalytically oriented psychotherapy, with its emphasis on unconscious purpose, as to religion (although the hidden power – God – is often construed as residing outside a person; but then access to the inner world of object relations usually depends first on interacting with people outside ourselves). Moreover, the history of institutionalized psychotherapy can be viewed as a process of constructing absolute belief systems, dissent from which has resulted in people leaving the movement they grew up in to form their own 'church'. Conversely, the pastoral work of many priests is very much less concerned with purveying any sense of absolute truth than helping people wrestle with their individual beliefs, personal realities and relative values.

Symington (1994) draws a distinction between primitive and mature religions in terms of whether the mental state of the believer is principally concerned with relating to external or internal forces. He contrasts behaviour such as the offering of sacrifices to appease potentially vengeful spirits, with activity directed towards enhancing the authenticity – and hence freedom – of the self. Religion and psychotherapy can exist in both primitive and mature states of mind.

Outlining differences and similarities between relative and absolute values in this way echoes the tensions between individual and collective interests described earlier. At different times, the emphasis moves away from the collective to the individual, or from the individual to the collective. What endures is the tension between the two. So it is that we can read novels written in the last century, or in the early part of this century, and recognize ourselves in the characters and situations depicted there (see Chapter 6). We can watch plays such as Ibsen's *The Doll's House* and find that, despite the portrayal of a world that existed in the Norway of 1879, the marriage of Nora and Torveld echoes themes that continue to be relevant to couples today. The conventional marriage based on man as protector and women as protected, concealing his dependence on her and her competence in relation to him, surviving until pressures from without and within combine to test to destruction the unconscious phantasy that both binds them together and drives them apart, and which leaves partners with a choice between having a *real* marriage or no marriage at all, is, as intimated in Chapter 10, a theme of archetypal significance.

At the present time the private dimensions of marriage are emphasized more than the public. Couples struggle to identify themselves as a partnership, and themselves within the partnership, in a social context that no longer imposes upon them the straitjacket of convention. This is profoundly liberating. It can also be profoundly difficult. Choice can complicate commitment, and it carries with it a burden of responsibility that individuals cannot disown.

The Shift From Rights to Responsibilities

The shift from public rights to private responsibilities, and its impact on relationships between men and women over the past three centuries, was outlined in Chapter 2 in the content of emerging divorce in England and Wales. Today there are now proposals for reforming divorce law in ways that move away from a preoccupation with adjudicating over the grounds for divorce and towards helping those who have decided to end their marriage to address the consequences of that decision (Law Commission, 1993). This mirrors a broader preference for resolving family conflict through private ordering rather than through public adjudication, a preference which has fuelled the mediation movement in Britain over the past two decades (Fisher, 1990).

The 1989 Children Act similarly emphasises the responsibilities of parents rather than their rights, and seeks to dissuade the judicial system from intervening in family life except where it is clearly necessary to do so. Even between couples, the 1991 Law Lords ruling reinstating the offence of rape within marriage – while attending to the rights of married women – reflects a movement towards reframing family relationships in ways that replace notions of property and ownership with relational values. As far as the couple goes, the economic and sexual emancipation of women, which has provided them with a greater measure of control over income and fertility than in the past, has encouraged marriage to be regarded as a relationship about which there can be choices, rather than an institution in which there are only obligations.

One of the dilemmas we face as family members and citizens is balancing individual needs and choices with our commitments and responsibilities to others. Marriage is a major commitment. So, too, is parenthood. The great majority of those marrying for the first time will expect to have children and succeed in doing so. Indeed, as we have seen earlier, children may provide a primary reason for marriage. It is hardly surprising, then, that children constitute the locus of concern when marriages end in divorce. Very few would argue that the commitment to children is other than a lifetime one, whereas the commiment to marriage may be seen as transitory. Public anxiety often clusters round the financial implications of divorce, fearing that private choices result in unacceptably high social costs. But the concern goes deeper than that.

One consequence of divorce is that in Britain, around 160,000 children a year are witnessing the break-up of partnerships which they regard as being vital to their own security. Over two million children are living in lone-parent households, the majority of them as a result of separation and divorce, and facing the emotional, social, economic and educational disadvantages that so often afflict these families. Many other children are brought up in newly-constituted family groupings, the boundaries of which are not defined by the family home. Although research reports are mixed, they do not, on the whole, paint an optimistic picture of the future for these children – especially, and perhaps surprisingly, when their parents remarry (Burghes, 1994). The pathways explaining these outcomes are diverse, involving psychological, economic and social factors which disallow any simple linkage between cause and effect.

The lessons children may learn from divorce are that others cannot be relied upon, that conflict results in the severance of relationships, and that their own thoughts and feelings are destructive and capable of bringing about catastrophe. Divorce may cost them the parent who has gone away, the stimulus and support of the parent who remains, a positive self-esteem broken by self-doubt and recrimination, and the material resources that provide a good start in life. This, admittedly, is the negative side of the picture. There are good outcomes from divorce as well, just as there are bad outcomes from families in which the parents have sustained a poor marriage. The question is: are parents to be held solely responsible for what happens in families, or are we as a community responsible for making matters worse by providing an environment which can undermine stability and continuity in relationships while offering little assistance to those who have to make the resulting changes?

Four assertions can be made about marriage, which emphasize the responsibilities couples take on when they marry. Each is supported by research and clinical experience.

- the capacity of people to sustain partnerships in adult life is significantly influenced by the models of partnership they internalize as children;
- the quality of partnerships is an important indicator of how well

men and women operate as parents, and this is true whether they live together or apart;

- the attitudes and support of the wider community is highly relevant to the success of both partnering and parenting enterprises;
- partnership is riddled with contradiction and paradox.

Partnership and Paradox

Marriage is full of paradox and contradiction, especially viewed against the backdrop of social change. There can be no tolerance and enjoyment of apartness in relationships without a fully consummated sense of togetherness. There can be no satisfying and stimulating close relationship with another person without a secure sense of being a separate person. Intimacy is founded on the capacity to be alone; the capacity to be alone stems from satisfactory involvements with others. As couples eschew marriage to form their own private contracts, pressure builds up for these individual contracts to be formally articulated and witnessed in law. The more intensely private people become in their marriages, the less of a window they have on the domestic lives of others, the more than usually susceptible they may be to images presented to them of 'normal' married life. Even when couples pursue their private dreams by leaving marriage to form a new partnership they may, in consequence, be faced more than ever before with the collective issues of family life: stepfamilies are more generously defined than traditional two-generational nuclear families, and must manage a complex web of open relationships. As the pendulum swings towards individualism, the reverse thrust towards collectivism is given added momentum.

The contradictions inherent in contemporary marriage are well illustrated by the different contributors in this book. The more emphasis that is placed on companionate values in marriage, the more likely it is to fail (see Chapter 5). There are deep contradictions between the premium placed by women on a 'common life' – or by men on a 'life in common' – (Mansfield and Collard, 1988) and the desire for individual autonomy that our culture values so highly, especially when the desire for openness in marriage can result in greater secrecy (Reibstein and Richards, 1992). There are contradictions in a climate that expects people to be sexually experienced before marriage and provides ready opportunities for sexual liaisons outside marriage, and the sexually exclusive, monogamous values that demarcate marriage from other relationships as powerfully today as they ever did (see Chapter 7). There are contradictions between the romantic ideals that make cohabitation attractive to some couples who, nevertheless, marry because of economic realities (see Chapter 8). And there are contradictions in the fact that marriage is increasingly being linked with having children and the fact that many couples are less satisfied with their partnership once they become parents.

Some of the conflicts and contradictions in marriage are relatively new, or, at least, are given extra prominence by the conditions of the day. Most are not, and have featured in other marriages at other times in history. Marriage without conflict is an illusion. Indeed, a manageable amount of conflict is necessary for both the relationship and the institution to develop. A good marriage, arguably the principal attachment relationship in adult life, balances the need for security and safety with the need for exploration and adventure. It balances a longing to be together with a drive to be apart. It enables one partner to be a part of the other and yet distinctly him or herself. Marriage then functions in terms that Bowlby (1988) might have described as a *secure base*. As a vitally important aspect of the psychological and social environment of the majority of people at some point in their lives, marriage is a statement of identity – for better and for worse. As such it creates opportunities for personal growth, development and fulfilment, as well as exposing partners to the dangers of atrophy, dissatisfaction and despair.

These opportunities and dangers apply not only to the private level of a couple's relationship but also to the public dimension of a community's social, cultural and economic life. As an open system, the *private* world of marriage both affects and is affected by the environmental context in which couples live out their lives. As an open system, the *public* world of marriage both affects and is affected by the personalities of the individuals who, together, constitute the couple. Marriage bridges individuals and the community of which they are a part; traffic crosses the bridge in both directions. When marriage works well there is mutual benefit; when it works badly there is mutual cost. Insofar as it fails to realise its purpose, the responsibility lies not just with individuals, or just with society, but in the relationship between the two. Moreover, marital failure – if that is the right phrase to use – represents in the relationship between men and women no more and no less than an unacknowledged need for change or an inability to bring it about. As a dynamic institution, marriage must change over time to meet the different demands and challenges of the day. This is as true for the institutionalized arrangements that bind couples together at different times in history as it is for the life course of a particular partnership.

Marriage is, then, both a personal and a political concern. Through it, models of partnership between women and men are transmitted to the next generation, lending it great significance for our future social ecology. One way or another, marriage will herald in the new millennium. Whether the result is transformation or tradition remains to be seen. This book has outlined some of the contradictions between image and reality that face men and women in marriage today, contradictions which are capable of fashioning something new when held in tension with one another. No blueprint is offered for the future. What is needed is an environment that is sufficiently sustaining for the work to go on.

Christopher Chulow

References

Ablon, J., 'The Significance of Cultural Patterning for the "Alcoholic Family" '. *Family Process* **19**, pp.127–144, 1980.

Anderson, R. S., and Guernsey D. B., *On Being Family: A Social Theology of the Family*. Michigan: Eerdmans, 1985.

Archbishop of Canterbury's Group on the Divorce Law, *Putting Asunder. A Divorce Law for Contemporary Society*. London: SPCK 1966.

Ashford, S. and Timms, N., *What Europe Thinks: A Study of Western European Values*. Aldershot: Dartmouth 1992.

Askham, J., *Identity and Stability in Marriage*. Cambridge: Cambridge University Press 1984.

Atkinson, D., *To Have and to Hold*. London: Collins 1979.

Bannister, K. and Pincus, L., *Shared Phantasy in Marital Problems: Therapy in a Four-Person Relationship*. London Institute of Marital Studies 1965.

Baring, A. and Cashford, J., *The Myth of the Goddess: Evolution of an Image*. London: Viking 1991.

Bateson, G., *Naven*. Stanford: Stanford University Press 1958.

Becker, G., *Treatise on the Family*. Cambridge: Harvard University Press 1974.

Berger, P. and Kellner, H., 'Marriage and the Construction of Reality', *Diogenes* **1**(23) 1964.

Bernstein, B., *Class, Codes and Control*. London: Routledge and Kegan Paul 1974.

Blumstein, P. and Schwartz, P., *American Couples*. NY: McGraw Hill 1983.

Bott, E., *Family and Social Networks*. London: Tavistock 1957.
'Family and Crisis'. In J. Sutherland (ed.), *Towards Community Mental Health*. London: Tavistock 1971.

Bowlby, J., *A Secure Base: Clinical Applications of Attachment Theory*. London: Routledge 1988.

Britten, V., *Halcyon or the Future of Monogamy*. London: Hutchinson 1929.

Britton, R., 'The Missing Link: Parental Sexuality in the Oedipus Complex'. In J. Steiner (ed.), *The Oedipus Complex Today: Clinical Implications*. London: Karnac Books 1989.

Burghes, L., *Lone Parenthood and Family Disruption*. London: Family Policy Studies Centre 1994.

Burgoyne, J., 'Does the Ring Make Any Difference?' In D. Clark (ed.), *Marriage, Domestic Life and Social Change*. London: Routledge 1991.

Cancian, F., 'The Feminization of Love'. *Signs: Journal of Women in Culture and Society*. **2** (4), pp.692–709, 1986.

Central Statistical Office, *Social Trends*. **23**, London: HMSO 1993.

Churton Braby, M., *Modern Marriage and How to Bear It*. London: Werner Laurie c. 1909.

Clulow, C., *Marital Therapy: An Inside View*. Aberdeen: Aberdeen University Press 1985.

Clulow, C. (ed.), *Rethinking Marriage: Public and Private Perspectives*. London: Karnac Books 1993.

Clulow, C. and Mattinson, J., *Marriage Inside Out: Understanding Problems of Intimacy*. Harmondsworth: Penguin 1989.

Colman, W., 'Marriage as a Psychological Container'. In S. Ruszczynski (ed.), *Psychotherapy with Couples*. London: Karnac 1993.

Comfort, A., *The Joy of Sex*: London: Quartet Books 1974.

De Rougemont, D., *Love in the Western World or Passion and Society*. NJ: Princeton University Press (1939) 1983.

Diamond, J., *The Rise and Fall of the Third Chimpanzee*. London: Radius 1991.

Dicks, H., *Marital Tensions*. London: Routledge and Kegan Paul 1967.

Dormor, D. J., *The Relationship Revolution*. London: One Plus One 1992.

Edgell, S., *Middle-Class Couples*. London: Allen and Unwin 1980.

Ehrenberg, M., *Women in Prehistory*. London: British Museum Publications 1989.

Eichenbaum, L. and Orbach, S., *Outside-In Inside-Out: A Feminist Psychoanalytic Approach to Women's Psychology*. Harmondsworth: Penguin Books 1982.

   What Do Women Want: Exploding the Myth of Dependency. London: Michael Joseph 1983.

Eliot, G., *Middlemarch*. London: Penguin Books 1982.

Elliott, B., 'Demographic Trends in Domestic Life', 1945–1987. In D. Clark (ed.), *Marriage, Domestic Life and Social Change*. London: Routledge 1991.

Engels, F., *The Origin of the Family, Private Property, and the State*. NY: Pathfinder Press (1884) 1974.

Erikson, E. H., *Childhood and Society*. Harmondsworth: Penguin Books 1956.

Falicov, C., 'Cultural Variations in the Family Life Cycle'. In E. A. Carter and M. McGoldrick (eds), *The Family Life Cycle: A Framework for Family Therapy*. NY: Gardner Press 1980.

Firth, R., *Essays on Social Organization and Values*. London: The Athlone Press 1969.

Fisher, E., *Woman's Creation: Sexual Evolution and the Shaping of Society*. NY: Anchor Press 1979.

Fisher, T., *Family Conciliation within the United Kingdom. Policy and Practice*. Bristol: Family Law 1990.

Freud, S., 'The Ego and the Id', SE XIX. London: Hogarth Press and the Institute of Psycho-Analysis 1923.

Freud, S., 'Group Psychology and the Analysis of the Ego'. SE XVIII. London: Hogarth Press (1921) 1950.

Galsworthy, J., *The Forsyte Saga*. London: Penguin Books 1978.

Gilmore, D. D., *Manhood in the Making: Cultural Concepts of Masculinity*. New Haven: Yale University Press 1990.

Gittins, D., *The Family in Question*. London: Macmillan 1985.

Goode, W. J., *World Changes in Divorce Patterns*. New Haven: Yale University Press 1993.

Gorer, G., *Sex and Marriage in England Today*. London: Nelson 1971.

Gosling, R., 'What is Transference?' In D. Sutherland (ed.), *The Psychoanalytic Approach*. London: Balliére, Tindall and Cassell 1968.

Graves, R., *The White Goddess; A Historical Grammar of Poetic Myth*. London: Faber & Faber 1961.

Greenson, R. R., 'Dis-identifying from mother: its special importance for the boy', *International Journal of Psycho-Analysis*. **49**, p.370, 1968.

Guirand, F. (ed.), *New Larousse Encyclopaedia of Mythology*. London: Hamlyn 1959.

Handy, C., *The Age of Unreason*. London: Hutchinson 1989.

Harris, M., 'The evolution of human gender hierarchies: a trial formulation'. In B. Miller (ed.), *Sex and Gender Hierarchies*. England: Cambridge University Press 1993.

Haskey, J., 'Premarital Cohabitation and the Probability of Subsequent Divorce: Analyses Using Data from the General Household Survey'. In *Population Trends* 68, London: HMSO 1992.

Hochschild, A., *The Managed Heart: The Commercialization of*

Human Feeling. Berkeley, CA: University of California Press 1983.

Hudson, L. and Jacot, B., *The Way Men Think: Intellect, Intimacy and the Erotic Imagination.* New Haven: Yale University Press 1991.

Jalmert, L., 'Increasing men's involvement as fathers in the care of children'. In *Men as Carers for Children.* Brussels: European Commission Childcare Network 1990 (available from the European Commission, (DGV/B/4) Rue de la Loi, B-1049 Brussels, Belgium).

Johnson, B., *Lady of the Beasts: Ancient Images of the Goddess and her Sacred Animals.* San Francisco: Harper & Row 1988.

Jones, E., 'Feminism and Family Therapy: Can Mixed Marriages Work?' In J. F. Perelberg and A. Miller (eds), *Gender and Power in Families.* London: Routledge 1990.

Joshi, H., *Motherhood and Employment.* London: OPCS 1987.

Jung, C. G., 'Marriage as a Psychological Relationship'. In *The Collected Works of C. G. Jung.* London: Routledge & Kegan Paul 1925.

Kiernan, K. and Estaugh, V., *Cohabitation: Extramarital childbearing and Social Policy.* London: FPSC 1993.

Kinsey, A., Pomeroy, W., Martin, C., and Gebhard, P., *Sexual Behaviour in the Human Male.* Philadelphia: W. B. Saunders 1948. *Sexual Behaviour in the Human Female.* Philadelphia: W. B. Saunders 1953.

Klein, M., 'Notes on Some Schizoid Mechanisms' (1946). In *The Writings of Melanie Klein*, **Vol.3**. London: Hogarth Press 1975.

Kraemer, S., 'The Origins of Fatherhood', *Family Process.*, **30**, pp.377–92, 1991.

Kraemar, S., 'What are Fathers For?' In C. Burck and B. Speed (eds.), *Gender, Power and Relationships: New Developments.* London: Routledge 1994.

La Fontaine, J., *Sex and Age as Principles of Social Differentiation.* ASA Monograph, **No. 17**. London: Academic Press.

Lamb, M., and Oppenheim, D., 'Fatherhood and father-child relationships: five years of research'. In S. Cath, A. Gurwitt and L. Gunsberg (eds), *Fathers and their Families.* NJ: The Analytic Press 1989.

Law Commission, *Looking to the Future: Mediation and the Ground for Divorce*, Cm. 2424, London: HMSO, 1993.

Lawson, A., *Adultery: An Analysis of Love and Betrayal.* Oxford: Oxford University Press 1990.

Lerner, G., *The Creation of Patriarchy*. NY and Oxford: Oxford University Press 1986.

Levi-Strauss, C., *The Elementary Structures of Kinship and Marriage*. Boston: Beacon Press (1949) 1969.

Structural Anthropology. London: Allen Lane 1968.

Lewis, C. and O'Brien, M., *Re-assessing Fatherhood: New Observations on Fathers and the Modern Family*. London: Sage 1987.

Maclean, M., *Surviving Divorce*. London: Macmillan 1991.

Mansfield, P. and Collard, J., *The Beginning of the Rest of Your Life*. London: Macmillan 1988.

Mattinson, J., 'Betrayal of Troth'. In S. Ruszczynski (ed.), *Psychotherapy With Couples*. London: Karnac Books 1993.

McGill, D. and Pearce, J. K., 'British Families'. In M. McGoldrick, J. Pearce and J. Giordano (eds), *Ethnicity and Family Therapy*. NY: The Guilford Press 1982.

McGoldrick, M. (ed.), *Ethnicity and Family Therapy*. NY: The Guilford Press 1982.

McRae, S., *Cohabiting Mothers*. London: Policy Studies Institute 1993.

Mead, M., *Male and Female*. Harmondsworth: Pelican 1962.

Mitchell, J., *Psychoanalysis and Feminism*. Harmondsworth: Penguin 1974.

Women: The Longest Revolution. London: Virago 1984.

Mooney, B., *From This Day Forward. An Anthology of Marriage*. London: Murray 1989.

Morley, R. E., *Intimate Strangers*. London: The Family Welfare Association 1984.

Neumann, E., *The Great Mother*. London: Routledge & Kegan Paul 1955.

Newson, E., and Newson, J., *Infant Care in an Urban Community*. London: Allen and Unwin 1963.

Four Years Old in an Urban Community. Harmondsworth: Penguin Books 1970.

Seven Years Old in the Home Environment. London: Allen and Unwin 1976.

O'Brien, M., *The Politics of Reproduction*. London: Routledge & Kegan Paul 1981.

Orbach, S., *Fat is a Femininist Issue*. London: Paddington Press 1978.

Paige, K. and Paige J., *The Politics of Reproductive Ritual*. Berkeley: University of California Press 1981.

Perelberg, R. J., 'Mental Illness, Family and Networks in a London Borough: Two Cases Studied by a Social Anthropologist'. *Social Science and Medicine* 17(8) pp.481–91, 1983.

Perelberg, R. J. and Miller, A. (eds), *Gender and Power in Families*. London: Routledge 1990.

Phillips, A., *The Trouble with Boys*. London: Pandora 1993.

Phillips, R., *Putting Asunder: A History of Divorce in Western Society*. Cambridge: Cambridge University Press 1988.

Pincus, L., (ed.), *Marriage: Studies in Emotional Conflict and Growth*. London: Institute of Marital Studies 1973.

Pruett, K. D., 'The Paternal Presence', *Families in Society: The Journal of Contemporary Human Services*. 74(1) pp.46–50, 1993.

Rapoport, R. and Rapoport, R. N., 'British Families in Transition'. In R. N. Rapoport, M. P. Fogarty and R. Rapoport (eds), *Families in Britain*. London: Routledge and Kegan Paul 1982.

Raschke, H., 'Divorce'. In M. Sussman and S. Steinmetz (eds), *Handbook of Marriage and the Family*. New York: Plenum Press 1987.

Redfearn, J., *The Exploding Self: The Creative and Destructive Nucleus of the Personality*. Il: Chiron Publications 1992.

Reibstein, J. and Richards, M., *Sexual Arrangements: Marriage and Affairs*. London: Heinemann 1992.

Richards, M. and Elliott, B., 'Sex and Marriage in the 1960s and 1970s'. In D. Clark (ed.), *Marriage, Domestic Life and Social Change*. London: Routledge 1991.

Rotunno, M. and McGoldrick, M., 'Italian Families'. In M. McGoldrick, J. Pearce and J. Giordano (eds), *Ethnicity and Family Therapy*. NY: The Guilford Press 1982.

Russell, G. and Radejovic, M., 'The Changing Role of Fathers? Current understandings and future directions for research and practice', *Infant Mental Health Journal*. 13, (4) pp.296–311, 1992.

Ruszczynski, S., 'Some Notes Towards a Psychoanalytic Understanding of the Couple Relationship', *Psychoanalytic Psychotherapy*, 6(1), pp.33–48, 1992.

'Thinking about and Working With Couples'. In S. Ruszczynski (ed.), *Psychotherapy with Couples*. London: Karnac Books 1993.

Sadgrove, M., 'Theological Images of Marriage'. In C. Clulow(ed.), *Rethinking Marriage: Public and Private Perspectives*. London: Karnac 1993.

Sanday, P., *Female Power and Male Dominance: On the Origins of Sexual Inequality*. Cambridge: Cambridge University Press 1981.

Sarsby, J., *Romantic Love and Society*. London: Penguin Books 1983.

Schofield, M., *The Sexual Behaviour of Young Adults*. London: Lane 1973.

Searles, H. F., *Collected Papers on Schizophrenia and Related Subjects*. London: Hogarth and the Institute of Psycho-Analysis 1955.

Senior, M., *The Illustrated Who's Who in Mythology*. London: Orbis/ Macdonald 1985.

Service, E., *Origins of the State and Civilization: The Processes of Cultural Evolution*. NY: W. W. Norton 1975.

Shon, S. P. and Davis, Y., 'Asian Families'. In M. McGoldrick, J. Pearce and J. Giordano (eds), *Ethnicity and Family Therapy*. NY: The Guilford Press 1982.

Spiegel, J. P., 'The Resolution of Role Conflict within the Family'. In M. Greenblatt (ed.), *The Patient and the Mental Hospital: Contributions of Research in the Sciences of Social Behaviour*. Il: Free Press 1957.

Symington, M., *Emotion and Spirit: Questioning the Claims of Pyschoanalysis and Religion*. London: Cassell 1994.

Tanner, N., *On Becoming Human*. Cambridge: Cambridge University Press 1981.

Temperley, J., 'Our Own Worst Enemies: Unconscious Factors in Female Disadvantage'. *Free Associations*, 1984.

Teruel, G., 'Considerations for a Diagnosis in Marital Psychotherapy', *British Journal of Medical Psychology* **39**(704) 1966.

Thomas, D., *Under Milk Wood*. London: J. M. Dent & Sons 1954.

Van de Valde, T. H., *Ideal Marriage: Its Physiology and Techniques*. London: Heinemann Books 1928.

Walker, B., *The Woman's Encyclopaedia of Myths and Secrets*. San Francisco: Harper & Row 1983.

Wellings, K., Field, J., Johnson, A. M., and Wadsworth, J., *Sexual Behaviour in Britain*. London: Penguin Books 1994.

Winnicott, D., 'Further Thoughts on Babies as Persons'. In *The Child, the Family and the Outside World*. Harmondsworth: Penguin Books 1964.

Winnicott, D. W., *The Maturational Processes and The Facilitating Environment*. London: Hogarth and the Institute of Psycho-Analysis 1965.

Wolfram, S., *In-Laws and Outlaws: Kinship and Marriage in England*. London: Croom Helm 1987.

Wright Mills, C. *The Sociological Imagination*. Oxford: Oxford University Press 1959.

Young-Eisendrath, P., *You're Not What I Expected*. NY: William Morrow 1993.

Index